THE

DINERS OUT VADE-MECUM

A POCKET HANDBOOK ON

THE MANNERS AND CUSTOMS OF SOCIETY FUNCTIONS
PUBLIC AND PRIVATE DINNERS, BREAKFASTS,
LUNCHEONS, AFTERNOON TEAS, AT-HOMES, RE-
CEPTIONS, BALLS AND SUPPERS, WITH HINTS
ON ETIQUETTE, DEPORTMENT, DRESS, CON-
DUCT, SELF-CULTURE, HEALTH, COURT-
SHIP AND MARRIAGE, AFTER-DINNER
SPEAKING, ENTERTAINMENT, STORY-
TELLING, TOASTS AND SENTIMENTS,
INDOOR AMUSEMENTS,
ETC., ETC., ETC.

BY

ALFRED H. MILES

Published in Great Britain in 2012 by Old House books & maps,
Midland House, West Way, Botley, Oxford OX2 0PH, United Kingdom.
44-02 23rd Street, Suite 219, Long Island City, NY 11101, USA.
Website: www.oldhousebooks.co.uk
© 2012 Old House

Every attempt has been made by the Publishers to secure the appropriate
permissions for materials reproduced in this book. If there has been any
oversight we will be happy to rectify the situation and a written submission
should be made to the Publishers.

A CIP catalogue record for this book is available from the British Library.

ISBN-13: 978 1 90840 235 6

Originally published c. 1925 by Stanley Paul & Co., Ltd.

Printed in China through Worldprint Ltd.
12 13 14 15 16   10 9 8 7 6 5 4 3 2 1

PREFATORY

THIS little book is an attempt to help the young and inexperienced to the reasonable enjoyment of the social pleasures of society by an elementary introduction to the rules and regulations which govern its functions, and a brief indication of the principles of chivalry and morality which underlie their enactment and exaction. It makes no claim to be a complete treatise on any one of the numerous subjects with which it incidentally deals, but its first word was written with the hope, and its last with the conviction, that it will serve a useful purpose by giving in a popular form, a great deal of suggestive information which may be pleasant and profitable to the reader, and through him to those with whom he may come in contact. Had more space been available the writer would have treated some subjects in greater detail, and have dealt with one or two others which might with some appropriateness have been included, but the inexorable limits of the reasonable pocket, which should never be allowed to disturb the symmetry of an exact fit, imposed conditions which could not be disregarded without danger to that perfect equipment which it is the book's object to promote. "Who's Who?" is a very comprehensive handbook of society nomenclature, but no fashionable tailor would undertake to accommodate it in the pocket of a dress-coat. Such as it is, the writer leaves his book in the reader's hands, hoping that it may be some small help to his enjoyment.

A. H. M.

INDEX

5

THE DINERS OUT
VADE-MECUM

DINNER is the most important as well as the most substantial meal of the day. It marks the meridian of gastronomic time, and all other meals are regulated by it. It offers the largest variety of food, and occupies the longest measure of time, and, if only on this latter account, deserves the most attention. In all ages feasting has been associated with both public and private rejoicing, and the evening meal has ever been the most esteemed. Abraham celebrated the weaning of Isaac with a great feast. "Laban gathered together all the men of the place and made a feast" to honour the marriage of Jacob, and Pharaoh kept his own birthday by giving a feast to his servants. Other occasions of the feasts of old were the consummation of the harvest and the vintage, the summer and the winter solstice. The Roman feast was always a supper, and commonly commenced at about three o'clock in the afternoon. These were often great occasions, and were protracted to a late hour. Julius Cæsar once gave entertainment to 22,000 guests, and the feast was enlivened by music, dancing, and gladiatorial exhibitions. The feasts of the Hebrews were varied by music, poetry, story-telling and the solution of riddles. It is interesting to note how many of these old customs survive in our modern practices.

DINERS may be classified as diners-in and diners-out. The diner-in is the host who gives the dinner, and in the majority of cases the guests are those who in their turn are diners-in, and who on such occasions reciprocate his hospitality. Besides these, however, there are others, bachelors and spinsters, visitors from abroad, or from a distance, who are welcomed for a variety of reasons, and from whom no invitation is expected in return. It is to these latter, and especially to the bachelors, that this little book is addressed.

ETIQUETTE is the accepted code of manners observed by good society. Its object is not restraint, but graceful freedom.

To be entirely at one's ease, without impairing the complete ease of others, is to secure the whole purpose and intent of etiquette.

He who has mastered the golden rule, " As ye would that others should do unto you, do ye unto them," has acquired the true spirit of etiquette, though he may yet have much to learn as to its application to the various experiences of life.

Like the laws of art, the laws of etiquette are deduced from the principles and practices observed by the best masters, and, like communal laws, they came into being in the first instance for the protection of the weak. It was to protect the weak against the strong of the community that communal laws were first enacted, and modern etiquette is an outcome and a survival of the olden spirit of chivalry, which led the brave to deserve the fair. To this day the gentleman is always presented to the lady, however noble his rank may be, and however lowly hers, and this is not done until it has been ascertained that the introduction will be agreeable to her.

Indiscriminate introductions are a sure sign of vulgarity, and no introduction should ever be made without the assurance that it will be agreeable to both parties.

The whole practice of good manners is based upon the gracious bearing of the higher to the lower in the social scale, and the equally gracious recognition of the accepted order of precedence on the part of the lower to the higher. When these obtain, both meet upon a common ground of practical understanding, without loss of dignity on either part.

Some of the earliest and best rules of etiquette may be traced to the early Christian writings and one lesson given in St. Luke xiv. 8-11 is so applicable to the diner-out to-day, that we venture to quote it here.

" When thou art bidden of any man to a marriage feast, sit not down in the chief seat ;

lest haply a more honourable man than thou be
bidden of him, and he that bade thee and him
shall come and say to thee, 'Give this man
place'; and then thou shalt begin with shame
to take the lowest place. But when thou art
bidden, go and sit down in the lowest place :
that when he that hath bidden thee cometh,
he may say to thee, 'Friend, go up higher :
then shalt thou have glory in the presence of
all that sit at meat with thee. For every one
that exalteth himself shall be humbled ; and he
that humbleth himself shall be exalted."

"In honour preferring one another" is also a
time-honoured maxim which may well be observed in general practice.

For special occasions, special laws are laid
down, and these should be duly observed; but
circumstances will often arise when it may be
difficult to apply any specific rule, and these
will be found to be the real opportunities and
tests of good manners. To break a law of
etiquette may be the misfortune of many not
well versed in the procedure of good society, or
new to the particular experience in passing; but
in such cases it is always the duty of the master
of deportment to observe the spirit which under-
lies all laws of good behaviour by refusing to.
be perturbed by untoward incident, and declining
to accentuate awkwardness at the expense of
the offender. To observe the laws of etiquette
is to act at least after the manner of a gentleman, but to intentionally humiliate another
who has unfortunately transgressed is to display
the spirit of a cad.

ROYAL MANNERS.—A certain architect un-
accustomed to association with royalty was once
called upon, in the pursuit of his professional
duty, to hand a silver trowel to H.M. King
Edward VII., at that time Prince of Wales,
in order that he might "well and truly lay" a
certain foundation-stone. The architect was
an extremely nervous man, and looked forward
with some trepidation to the, to him, formidable
ordeal. His fears, however, were quite illusory.
He was dealing with a master of deportment,
who immediately on his arrival at the scene of
the ceremonial, sent for him, complimented him
upon the designs he had prepared for the building
about to be erected, and put him so entirely at

his ease that the function became a pleasure instead of a pain.

An equal instance of gracious bearing and true delicacy of feeling is recorded of Queen Alexandra, who on one occasion was taking tea with the wife of a provincial mayor, when, from careful habit, the mayoress placed a lace handkerchief across her knees. Some of the court ladies present observed the act, and smiled their superiority, the one to the other. The Queen noticed both the act and the inaudible comment, and taking her own handkerchief followed the suit of the mayoress, thus putting her hostess entirely at her ease, to the inward discomfort of the ladies of her suit. It was ever so : the best people are always the most easy to deal with.

PERFECT BREEDING.—Daniel Webster, referring to English manners, said : " The rule of politeness in England is to be quiet, act naturally, take no airs, and make no bustle. This perfect breeding has cost a great deal of drill." There are no surer signs of vulgarity than loud talking, fussy behaviour, and obtrusive conduct, whether upon the part of the entertainer or the entertained. Ostentation on the one part and aggressiveness on the other are equally to be deprecated. Wealth, rapidly acquired nowadays, often places small men in large positions, and thus opens the door of hospitality, without having first graduated host and hostess in the art of entertainment. This leads to mixed gatherings, and often ill-assorted associations. And these cannot always be avoided. To maintain one's own self-respect, without hurting the feelings of others, by observing quietly, amid unconventional surroundings, the refinements and manners of good society must be the aim of the gentleman.

FORMAL INTRODUCTIONS, as we have already seen, are never made unless it is known that they will be agreeable to both parties, and in all cases the gentleman is introduced to the lady. But this does not prevent informal introductions being made on occasion for temporary purposes. At a dinner party the guests are selected by the host and hostess on the intelligent assumption that they will be agreeable to each other. In such cases it would not be polite of either party to refuse an introduction, but such introductions need not involve lifelong acquaintance, and do not really survive the occasion for which they are made. As elsewhere stated, in such cases the parties bow, but do not shake hands. Introductions made in a ballroom are of the same character, and follow the same usage. The gentleman introduced for the purpose of a dance offers the lady his right arm, and conducts her to the floor of the room. There are, however, introductions which involve the shaking of hands, as when one is introduced to the relations of one's *fiancé*. These are assumed to be the beginnings of lifelong friendships, and so are inaugurated with more of heartiness and less of formality. Sometimes persons unfamiliar with polite usage desire, for the gratification of their own vanity, introductions to the more distinguished persons present, and these often place others in a very awkward position by asking them to effect such introductions on no other ground than that the person asked is on terms of friendship with both parties. In such cases the person whose kindly offices are requested may, if a man of resource, be trusted to act with discretion towards both friends. He may judge from his knowledge of the two whether the introduction would be agreeable or not, and decline or further it, or he may make direct inquiries and act accordingly.

If the third person is agreeable to the introduction, the difficulty is at an end, but if he declines it, some tact is required on the part of the intermediary in dealing with the proposer, who is often enough one not quick to understand a delicate hint. Persons seeking introductions and not receiving any encouragement should accept the fact as an indication that the proposal is not acceptable, but if too dull to take the hint for a definite reply, there is no alternative but to remind the inquirer that it is a rule of English society only to introduce persons upon the assurance that the introduction will be agreeable to both parties, and to add, " For some reason which he has not given, or best known to himself, Mr. So-and-so does not desire it." Persons seeking introductions should also remember that similar consideration is due from them to the friend whose kindly offices they seek

to employ. No one ought to be asked to introduce two persons unless the one seeking the
introduction feels sure that the office will be
agreeable to the intermediary. All these points
of delicacy are accentuated when the persons
proposed for introduction are of opposite sex.

SHAKING HANDS is one of the most characteristic actions of common life, and there is perhaps
no action to which more character can be im-
parted. All kinds of eccentricity find expression
in the hand-shake, and that is probably why
society has reduced the practice to somewhat
formal limits. We all know the "pump-handle"
shake, and the "concertina" shake, and the
"piston" shake needs no description. Most of
us can recall hand-shakes which are combina-
tions or mixtures of all these. The saving merit
of these greetings is their undoubted sincerity.
Then come the hand-shakes, if they may be so
called, which indicate the various degrees of
indifference and contempt with which conscious
superiority patronises its betters, and the
"vice" hand-shake, which crushes the hand of
the inexperienced and unexpectant, to the amusement of the cad who inflicts the torture. Besides
these there are the three degrees of altitude at
which the shake, or what passes for a shake, may
be made, and which may be described as the
front-door altitude, the first-floor altitude and
that of the top flat. All extremes are vulgar,
and society generally adopts the middle course.
Extremes may be represented by—

> " the true good-hearted shake
> Of friendship's hand for friendship's sake,
> When love's deep power nerves the arm,
> And strength meets strength as palm greets palm."

And,

> "The flabby lump of flesh and bone,
> That one may shake or leave alone :
> An insult in a friendly way
> Unfit to scare a crow away."

There are, of course, occasions when the hand
should be shaken, and occasions when it should
not; but it may be taken as certain that if the
hand is offered it should be accepted, as to refuse
it would have the appearance of a slight.

INVITATIONS are issued by the hostess in
the name of the host and herself, and the

reply should be addressed to both. If the party is to be a small one, the invitations are usually made in writing, but where this would involve the hostess in too much labour, cards, such as are procurable at any fancy stationer's, are used. They should be issued not too long in advance, and yet sufficiently early to facilitate the convenience of both parties, and to anticipate prior engagements. The larger the party, the longer the notice, is a convenient rule. In the ordinary way, a fortnight is regarded as a reasonable notice, though sometimes a month or more is given. The longer period, though fashionable, is to be deprecated, as it limits the liberty of the guest in a way which may easily become embarrassing. A week or ten days is usually considered sufficient notice for a small dinner party.

An invitation to dinner is a compliment paid, and demands a correspondingly courteous response. It may, of course, be accepted or declined, but whether the one or the other, the decision should be communicated without delay. It is due to the hostess who is to provide the entertainment that she should know as soon as possible for whom, and for how many, she has to provide. Guests who keep hostesses long in doubt as to their intentions, and who at the last moment, as it were, send their regrets, are quite likely, and deservedly so, to find their names removed from the guest-list of the house. Acceptances or regrets should be written in the third person and sent as soon as possible after the receipt of the invitation.

DRESS known as **Evening Dress** should always be worn at formal dinner parties. The dinner jacket is not admissible except on informal occasions. **The Tail Coat** with black trousers and boots or shoes and a white or black tie are the proper equipment. **Double Collars** should not be worn with evening dress, though they are admissible with dinner jackets and other informalities at home, and on informal occasions. **Dinner Jackets** may be worn by parties of gentlemen dining or visiting theatres, but must never be worn at a formal dinner, at the opera, or at a ball. In private the presence of ladies would seem to mark the distinction, though at home the ladies are inclined to allow the gentlemen more latitude than they enjoy abroad.   **Waistcoats** may be black or white as the guest may determine, but a white waistcoat should be without pattern, ornament, or decoration. The practice of wearing coloured **Handkerchiefs** tucked in the bosom of the waistcoat has been vulgarised out of use. **A White Handkerchief** in the breast pocket is the right thing in the right place. The practice of tucking the handkerchief up the coat sleeve as copied from military habit is to be deprecated. It has a slovenly appearance, though it is copied from the smart service. **Watch Chains** are taboo in evening dress, whether the waistcoat be black or white, but why it is difficult to understand. Evening dress is sombre enough under any circumstances, and might well be allowed this little alleviation, though, of course, all display of jewellery is vulgar. A silk ribbon, or perhaps a fine hair chain may pass if it be black. For outdoor wear, collapsible **Opera Hats** are the most approved headgear, with a **Light Overcoat** or heavier as may suit the requirements of the weather. Men are sometimes seen in the streets at the West End of London with no covering over their evening dress, but it looks loud, and is therefore not good form.   **Gloves** should be worn for the protection of the hands, but of a quiet colour, and suitable to the season of the year. The bachelor, as a rule, is not a carriage man, and if the evening be fine, and the distance short, he may with all propriety walk to the house of his host. Should he do so, he must take care, if he turns up the legs of his trousers before starting, to turn them down again before entering the reception-room. If he has worn heavy gloves out of doors, he will also take the first opportunity of substituting the light ones suitable for the reception. He should not offer his hostess a glove which has been handling a cane or an umbrella, twirling a moustache, or manipulating a cigar.

PUNCTUALITY should be observed in all things, and invitations to dinner usually indicate the limits within which the guest is free to suit his own convenience. Fifteen or more minutes, according to the number of guests expected, is usually allowed for the reception, and an invitation for seven o'clock commonly means dinner at

7.15. To delay a dinner is a crime, for which no adequate punishment has yet been discovered.

Beranger, the poet, once gave it as a reason for his invariable practice of being punctual at dinner that waiting guests usually occupy the interim in discussing the faults of the absentee. Those who desire to stand well with all concerned will do wisely to follow the poet's example.

Failure in this particular on the part of a guest is a slight upon those who are seeking to do him honour. It is the guest's duty to present himself to his hostess in the most approved form possible to him. His dress should fulfil all the conditions already indicated, and should be of good material, make, and fit ; and should bear no mark of haste or carelessness in dressing, or exposure to dust and weather in transit. Let him remember that he has his part to play in the success of the evening, and that it is due to his host and hostess that he should play it well, and so, having dressed himself properly for his part, let him present himself in good time, spick and span as a confection from a band-box if he likes, but free, severely free, from the atmosphere of the made up.

THE RECEPTION.—On arrival, the servants will assist in the removal, and take charge of the out-door garments, and on reaching the reception-room will announce entrance. The guest will immediately approach and shake hands with his hostess, and then his host. If he is accompanied by a lady, she will precede him at the reception. In no case should they either approach the room, or enter it, arm-in-arm, Having shaken hands with the host and hostess, and passed a few words with them, the guest will naturally look round the room for any he may expect to see, or any with whom he is on friendly terms. If these are near, he may with propriety shake hands with them, but if at a distance, a slight bow is a sufficient recognition. It is during the reception that the host and hostess make what introductions are necessary, and among these the introductions of those who are to accompany each other to the dinner table. The gentleman will in all cases be introduced to the lady, to whom he will bow, but with whom he will not shake hands. A few words of easy conversation should now break the ice, and prepare the way for the larger opportunity of conversation at the dinner table, after which he will in due course give his right arm to her, and according to the precedence indicated by the hostess, conduct her to the dining-room. Should the passage to the dining-room involve a staircase with the wall on the left hand, the gentleman will give the lady the left arm, that she may take the inside position, as she would were they walking out-of-doors. On the announcement that dinner is served, made by the butler, the host gives his right arm to the principal lady guest, and proceeds to lead the way to the dining-room, followed by the guests, whose order of precedence is regulated by the hostess, who brings up the rear on the right arm of the principal male guest. The seats allotted to the individual guests are usually indicated by cards, bearing their names, or are pointed out as they enter by the host, who, as a rule, remains standing until all are seated. Should it so happen that unavoidable circumstances detain the guest until after the company have gone in to dinner, the servants will conduct him direct to the dining-room, and it will be his duty to make his way straight to his hostess, shake hands with, and apologise to her, and then proceed to his seat with as little fuss and confusion as possible. An apology to the lady who was deprived of her escort by his late arrival would not be out of place. When all are seated the host will be found to occupy the bottom of the table with the principal lady guest on his right and the hostess will preside at the head of the table, with the principal gentleman guest on her left. If the guest is a novice it will become him to avoid prominence, and to watch from unobserved retirement the actions of others. He will have no difficulty in following the due observances of society, if he observes the course taken by those more experienced than himself, and conforms to general usage. Let him in all cases preserve a calm self-possession, and never under any circumstances act in a hurry.

GRACE BEFORE MEAT is pronounced at the desire of the host by some clergyman who may be present, or by himself.   In either case the

simplest form is the best. " Benedictus, bene-
dicat. Amen," is perhaps the briefest. "For
what we are about to receive, may the Lord
make us truly thankful" is perhaps the most
simple and informal. "Sanctify, O Lord, these
mercies to our use and us to Thy service," is
another well-known and often-used grace, while
the following well-known collect is admirably
available for almost any function which custom
regards as suitably opened with prayer. "Prevent us, O Lord, in all our doings with Thy
most gracious favour, and further us with Thy
continual help, that in all our works begun,
continued, and ended in Thee, we may glorify
Thy holy Name, and finally by Thy mercy
obtain everlasting life ; through Jesus Christ
our Lord. Amen."

At rural gatherings where grace is sometimes
sung the old quatrain may still serve :

> "Be present at our table, Lord ;
> Be here and everywhere adored ;
> These mercies bless, and grant that we
> May feast in paradise with Thee."

That laymen are often called upon to say
grace, lest it should be omitted altogether, is the
reason why we cite these examples here. There
are few things more unpleasant than to be nonplussed before others, whether in private or
public, and there is no reason why the simple
act of saying grace before meat should embarrass
any one. The Earl of Selkirk once called upon
Robert Burns to say grace, and the Selkirk grace
is well worthy of inclusion among these examples.

> "Some ha'e meat and canna eat,
> Some wad eat that want it ;
> We ha'e meat, and we can eat,
> And sae the Lord be thankèt."

How extremely embarrassing it may be to be
called upon to pray in public was shown some
time ago in the case of two well-known barristers,
one of whom, a prominent Nonconformist, was
accustomed to preach occasionally while on
circuit. His learned friend, who was a wit and a
caricaturist, could not, on one occasion, resist
the temptation to go and hear him. The preacher
seeing the gay Q.C. in one of the foremost pews,
did not relish the idea of preaching in the presence
of his quizzical friend, so, announcing the hymn
to be sung before the sermon, he added the words,

" After the singing of the hymn, Brother Lock-
wood will lead us in prayer." Brother Lock-
wood was quite nonplussed by this announcement. The pulpit had completely turned the
tables upon him, and during the singing of the
hymn, he lost no time in retiring.

An amusing story is told of Compton, the
actor, who on a certain occasion when travelling
in the country, called at a village inn and
ordered refreshment. Wearing a dress-suit
covered by a long black coat, which left his
white cravat exposed to view, he was mistaken
by the landlord for a clergyman, and was
introduced as such to a party of clerics who
were about to dine. Invited by a Dean, who
presided, to join the party, he was asked to
occupy the seat at the Dean's right hand, and
as a further compliment was requested to say
grace. There was no possibility of escape,
but, being accustomed to overcome stage fright,
he was able to rise to the occasion. Not quite
sure as to the formula he ought to use, he seized
upon the first idea that presented itself to him,
and said, in a rich, melodious voice : " O
Lord, open Thou our lips, and our mouths
shall show forth Thy praise."

THE MENU is printed for all public dinners,
and most private dinner parties of importance.
The variation is not great : *hors d'œuvres*,
soup, fish, entrées, joints, game, ice-pudding
and savouries, sweets and dessert follow with
time-honoured regularity, and host and hostess
are always pleased to see their guests do justice
to their hospitality. It need hardly be pointed
out that vulgarity has a loud voice and can
express itself in many ways, in few perhaps
more offensively than in eating and drinking.
Deportment without awkwardness, mastication
without noise, and satisfaction without re-
pletion is the desideratum. What to eat and
what to leave is a matter for individual discretion, and the printed menu gives a good
opportunity for selection. A famous French
cook once claimed that the whole of his menu
was arranged on scientific principles, and said
that he would not be responsible for the consequences to any diner who omitted any of
his courses. But appetites vary and digestions
differ, and the diner who finds that certain

dishes disagree with him is certain to disagree with the cook. "Know thyself" is a time-honoured maxim which needs to be remembered at the dinner table as elsewhere. **A well-ordered table** is a pretty sight, with its white cloth, its bright silver, and shining glass, to say nothing of the dainty flowers and the varicoloured fruit, which add so much to its adornment, and yet when one descends from the general to the particular, and squarely faces one's own small portion, it presents, at least to the novice, a somewhat formidable appearance. In the forefront he is faced with a dinner napkin folded maybe mitre-fashion, a loaf already in its mouth waiting the arrival of the fishes. On the left of his plate he will find a fair array of forks, and on the right a complementary equivalent of knives. There are probably more tools required daily for the feeding of a man's body than would be needed for its surgical dissection. The writer hopes that this thought will not impair the diner's appetite. The accompanying diagram shows the disposition of the tools required for the graceful disposal of the food included in a full menu. The number will lessen with the modification of the menu, and vary according to the character of the foods. If *hors d'œuvres* are included in the menu an additional knife and fork will be found upon the plate ready for use. The

knife beyond the plate is for butter or cheese, the spoon and fork for sweets, and the smaller spoon for ice. If oysters are included in the menu a tiny fork is often placed with its prongs turned upwards in the bowl of the soup spoon, and its handle lying diagonally across the outer knife and fish-knife.

Hors-d'œuvres are often placed upon the table that the guests may help themselves, at other times they are handed round as the other courses are, after the guests are seated. The second dish is **the soup**, of which there are many varieties, commonly differentiated as "thick" and "clear." The diner will of course choose according to his taste, but if he wears a heavy moustache he will probably discriminate. The soup spoon, which is the largest of the spoons used, will be found on the right hand of the plate. Soup should be eaten, like other courses, as served, subject to the moderate use of condiments. Small cruets are placed within easy reach of the diners, and should be used with discrimination. The ostentatious use of condiments is a reflection on the cook, and, through the cook, on the host and hostess. Bread, which should always be broken with the fingers, and not bitten off, should never be put into the soup but eaten separately. The plate may be tilted if necessary, but not towards the diner. To tilt it towards the outer edge allows any droppings which may fall from the spoon to reach the plate before the spoon is held to the lips. When dishes are handed round the one handed to a diner is intended for him, and should not be passed on, nor should the diner wait until the whole table is served. Second helpings of any course should not be asked for : it disturbs the service of the whole table When finished the spoon should be left in the plate with the bowl upwards. **Wines.**—Hosts differ and tastes vary, and in the matter of wines practice is much simpler than formerly. At table the servants will offer such choice of wines as may be suitable for each course. In response you either name the wine or point to the glass made for it. **With Oysters and Relishes** of all kinds, Vermouth, Sherry, Madeira, or Marsala may be taken. **With Soups and Fish** white wines, Rhine wine, Sauterne and light white Burgundies go well. **With Relêves or Entrées** clarets, red Bordeaux, red Hungarian

wine, red Swiss wine or Italian wines. So far,
the wines have been selected with a view to
stimulating appetite. Burgundy may be continued to be served throughout the dinner.
With Roasts champagne and other sparkling
wines are served. **With Coffee** Kirsch, brandy.
After Coffee liqueurs. Sherry is served with

1   2   3   4   5

soup, and a small glass is used (Fig. 1). **Glasses**
of various sizes, shapes, and colour are used for
the several classes of wines, and these are of
various designs. Hock, chablis, or sauterne
is served with fish, and a larger glass is used
(Fig. 2). Champagne comes round with the
joints or game, and a still larger glass is
commonly employed (Fig. 3). Though they
vary in shape, champagne glasses are always
the largest of the suite. Port is drunk with
dessert, and the smaller of the gobular-shaped
glasses is used (Fig. 4). Liqueurs are usually
served after the ice, and in the smallest glass
of all (Fig. 5). Claret and Burgundy are
served in the glass commonly used for hock ;
Madeira, and Marsala in the glass used for
sherry. Coffee is served last before, or first
after, the toast of "The King" at public
dinners, and after the departure of the ladies
at a private one. Counting the hors-d'œuvres
as a course, though it is only an appetiser,
Fish is the third course, and fish-knives and forks
are used. These will be found the first and last
of the formidable array on either side the plate.
All usual accessories are served with the several
courses, and it is safe to take anything or everything that is offered. As they are used, knives,
forks, and glasses are removed from the table,
and others, when required, are added. When
finished with, knives and forks should be
placed side by side on the plate, the blade of
the knife towards the fork, and the prongs of

the fork turned upwards. Plates are next served for **the entrées**, which are handed round in silver dishes, from which the diner helps himself. Serving oneself from one of these dishes sideways, as one has to do, is one of the awkwardnesses of dinner service which needs improving upon. Picking and choosing is equally open to suspicion whether done from motives of modesty or greed. While the practice lasts, however, it must be accepted and acted upon with as much grace as possible. The diner uses the spoon and fork in the entrée dish when serving himself to an entrée, and, except where a knife is really necessary, a fork only in eating it. Those who use the right tools for anything always find a smaller number sufficient. **Joints and game** follow, either as separate courses in sequence, or as alternative dishes simultaneously. With these the accessory vegetables, gravies, etc., are served. The *pièce de résistance* occupies the plate when placed upon the table, and the accessories are offered to the diner, who helps himself. **Sweets** follow the joints and game, and the fork, with the spoon in reserve, come on duty. The proper use of the spoon is not that of the knife which, if really needed, should be used. It has its own sphere, in which the fork cannot take its place, in dealing with soft-cooked fruits and ices for instance, but the fork is a much neater and more dainty implement for raising food to the lips, and, held in the right hand, may be made equal to most occasions. **Savouries** come next, and sometimes the fork requires the assistance of a knife, and sometimes both are dispensed with. Knives and forks are a product of modern civilisation, but "fingers were made before forks" we are sometimes told, and for certain purposes they are preferable to later devices. Bread broken by the fingers, or buttered is lifted to the mouth by them. Cheese-straws and other cheese served on a miniature tray of bread, are eaten in the same way. So are celery, asparagus, water-cress, and arti-chokes. **Dessert** brings the dinner to a close. It is ushered in by the laying of a dessert plate containing a doily, a finger-glass, and a dessert knife and fork. The diner removes the doily to his left hand, and places the bowl upon it, leaving the knife and fork on either side of his plate, and then selects the fruit he wishes to enjoy. **Fruit** needs very careful negotiation, and many prefer to leave it alone. Bananas, apples, pears, apricots, nectarines, and peaches all require peeling, and for this purpose a knife and fork should be used, as well as in eating them when peeled. Oranges are so pretty from a decorative point of view, and so difficult to treat experimentally, that it is better to leave them to the adornment of the dinner table, and negotiate more intimate relations with them at more convenient seasons. Fruits which require the removal of certain parts, such as grapes with their skins, cherries with their stones, strawberries with their stalks, are difficult to deal with, and some are better left, like oranges, for private consumption. Strawberries may be served with their stalks removed, or the diner may remove them with his fingers, and then using his fork dip them into the cream and sugar on his plate and raise them to his mouth. Raspberries may be dealt with in the same fashion, but few things look more unpleasant on a plate than a pile of ejected grape skins, cherry stones, and the like. It may be fastidious, but one has the feeling that anything which has been in the mouth and has to some extent been masticated, ought not to be seen on the plate again. The spoon may aid the fork in some of these matters, and in the case of crystallised fruits the knife must be called into play. Almonds and raisins and nuts may be manipulated with the fingers. The truth is, the simplest, neatest, and cleanest way of disposing of one's food is the one which most commends itself to refined acceptance.

TABLE TALK.—At dinner there are ample opportunities of conversation, and it is the duty of the diner-out to save his partner from *ennui* on the one hand and boredom on the other. The diner-out who exhausted his resources in a gallant attempt to interest his partner in the subject of cheese was scarcely a success, except as an example of the inept. It is an old story, but it is worth repeating as a classic illustration of heroic efforts under trying circumstances. "Do you like cheese?" was the first venture of this unfortunate young man, uttered in a subdued tone of voice, but only to elicit a negative reply. "Does your brother like cheese?" was the next inquiry after an impressive pause. "I have no brother," was the gentle response. Things were getting desperate, but our hero dared another query before he finally succumbed, "If you had a brother do you think he would like cheese?" This appears to have finished the conversation, for no answer is recorded. The gentleman in this case did his best to entertain the lady, and he probably succeeded, but scarcely after the manner of his intention.

THE ART OF CONVERSATION is not that of talking all the time. It is the art of drawing the best out of others, and contributing the best of one's own to the general treatment of the subject under discussion. Great talkers are not necessarily good conversationalists. Lord Macaulay was a man of vast and varied information. Sydney Smith said of him "He not only overflows with learning, but he stands in the slops," and another contemporary said in reference to him "I wish I was as cocksure of anything as Lord Macaulay is of everything." But these were not the qualities of a good conversationalist. Macaulay was a great talker, a fine orator; but conversation in the true sense was hardly possible in his presence. Samuel Taylor Coleridge was another example of those who, having great knowledge and being great talkers, kill conversation. "Did you ever hear me preach?" he once said to Charles Lamb, to which the wit replied, "I have never heard you do anything else."

TOPICS FOR CONVERSATION are never far to seek, nor difficult to pursue, and, given ordinary intelligence, it should be quite easy to open up subjects of mutual interest, amusement, or edification. **Places one has visited** during previous holidays spent at home or abroad often provide interesting topics of conversation, in which those who take part can compare notes and relate experiences, humorous and otherwise. **Books one has read** form another fruitful source of interesting conversation between intelligent companions, when interchanges of opinion on recent fiction, the latest biography, the last book of travel, the youngest and the sweetest of the poets may occupy pleasant intervals. **Plays one has seen**, and the comparative methods of different actors and actresses in the treatment of the same parts, is another subject of perennial interest, which may well do duty in killing time after the most approved society fashion. **Art and Artists**, the exhibitions of the Royal Academy, and the other societies of painters may form congenial subjects of conversation in some cases, while **Music and Musicians**, the first fiddler of the year, or the most lustrous star of the opera or the concert hall, may be the means of introducing an air with variations, which shall not fail of touching a sympathetic chord. **Sports, Pastimes, and Hobbies** all have their votaries, and a match at Lord's, a boat-race on the river, and such society gatherings as are represented by such words as Hurlingham, Ascot, and Henley, may serve to revive pleasant recollections and suggest interesting reminiscences, which may more than suffice the occasion. Ladies are much more interested in sport than they were formerly, and this opens a wide field for interesting conversation. **Politics** are best avoided, as differences of opinion should not be allowed to interfere with the social harmony of the hour, and even in gatherings of no more than two persons heated argument and embittered controversy are frequently the result of party discussion. **Public Men and Women** are fair objects of fair comment, and the men and women of one's common acquaintance may often be the pleasant subjects of pleasant remark, though the criticism of one's friends is always a delicate matter, and good taste, no less than good nature, demand tact and resource. Some people have an unhappy knack of placing their partners in very awkward positions when discussing common friends, and many an estrangement has followed upon a remark which should never have been made, or which, if made, should never have been repeated, and even the tacit acceptance of a remark which the hearer may not approve and may not care to controvert has been taken as an endorsement of the opinion expressed, and quoted as such with unhappy results. The desideratum under such circumstances is a sufficient tact and resource to steer the conversation into a new channel when rocks loom in the distance and breakers roar ahead.

TACT.—Some questions are much easier to answer than avoid, and yet wisdom demands that they shall be avoided at all hazards. Mr. Sims Reeves gives a good illustration of the tact required under some circumstances in his Jubilee volume of "Reminiscences." He tells us that the late Sir Michael Costa was in the habit of sending as a present to his friend Rossini, at Christmas time, a fine Stilton cheese in prime condition. After the production of his oratorio "Eli," Sir Michael sent the usual Stilton, but accompanied by a copy of the score of his new work. What passed between the two friends by way of criticism is not known, but it is recorded that a friend of Rossini's, anxious to hear his opinion, asked him what he thought of the oratorio. "The cheese was excellent," was his only reply. Kemble was once placed in a similar difficulty by a persistent critic, who questioned him as to his opinion of Mr. Conway, a young actor of his time. "Mr. Conway, sir ?" he said. "Well, Mr. Conway is a very tall young man." "Yes, of course, I know that," said the inquirer, "but what do you *think* of him ?" "Oh ! think of him, yes, exactly. I think," said the imperturbable actor, "Mr. Conway is a very tall young man." A similar story is told of a famous German 'cello player, who was interrogated as to the merits of a certain French violinist of his acquaintance. "He haf a verra fine insthrument," was the reply. "Ja, ja, I know zat is obvious, he haf a fine insthrument, but how does he blay ?" "Blay ? I tell you he haf a verra fine insthrument."

Reputations are not lost and actions for slander do not lie when people answer as discreetly as these professionals did. Let us hope the reader may never be involved in a difficulty of the kind, but if he is, to be forewarned is to be forearmed, and example is better than precept. The illustrations given will show an adroit manner of preserving the qualities of some very good friends from undue vivisection.

AWKWARD SITUATIONS will often arise from want of care in general conversation, and one cannot be too careful how one speaks of other persons in mixed company, for one never knows who may be within hearing of their remarks. According to a Stuttgart musical journal, several ladies and gentlemen were, on a certain occasion, travelling together in a railway carriage from Dresden to Leipsic. They were mostly strangers to each other, but the conversation soon became general. One lady, who had been present at a performance of " Euryanthe " at the Court Theatre the night before, passed some very severe strictures upon the production of the work. " Worse than all," she said, " that Madame Schröder is much too old for her part; her singing has become unbearable," and then turning to the gentleman sitting next her she said, " Do you not think so too ? " The gentleman looked somewhat amused, and then replied somewhat coldly, " Would you not rather tell all this to Madame Schröder herself ? She is sitting opposite to you." What the lady's feelings were must be left to the imagination ; but, recovering from her surprise, she turned to the singer with many confused apologies and said, " It is that horrid critic Schmieder who has influenced my judgment concerning your singing. I believe it is he who is always writing against you. He must be a most disagreeable and pedantic person." " Had you not better tell all this to Mr. Schmieder himself ? " calmly replied Madame Schröder. " He is sitting beside you." Two imaginations would hardly be equal to describing the lady's sufferings during the remainder of the journey.

In speaking of people who are absent, it is always best to observe the golden rule, and if there are no pleasant things that can be said about them, to remember that " the least said is soonest mended." As some writer has well said, We certainly owe it to our common humanity, to show the same consideration for men and women that we do for a picture, by taking care to look at them in the best light.

But conversation at dinner parties is not necessarily limited to two persons, and if the company be small and the story a good one, there is often no reason why all should not benefit by it. The direction of general conversation must always be left in the hands of the host, and it is simply rude for any guest, however distinguished, to monopolise it. A good host is, however, alert for the amusement of his guests, and if he sees a group evidently enjoying a good story, he may request that it shall be told for the benefit of the whole party. In such cases the story should be told to the host or hostess, that others may hear, but only at their request.

Loud Talking should be avoided, though when many are engaged in conversation it is sometimes difficult to make oneself heard, say, across the table by one's *vis-à-vis* without raising the voice. Perhaps the best rule is to avoid conversation that cannot be carried on without effort, and that leaves one open to the risk of a sudden cessation of the general conversation, throwing one's own vociferance into all too bold relief. A very amusing story may be told here, illustrating the awkwardness which may arise under such circumstances, and which may lead up to some remarks on telling stories which may perhaps be helpful to the diner-out. The story itself, though rather a difficult one to tell, if well told, never fails of great amusement.

Dr. M'Gregor of Edinburgh owned a parrot which was remarkable for the clearness and distinctness of its words. One of its sayings usually repeated after hearing any unusual sound was "Great Scott, M'Gregor, did you hear that?" At a dinner-party given by the doctor an elderly lady made a remark under the circumstances indicated above which attracted the parrot's attention, and who commented upon it in his usual formula, "Great Scott, M'Gregor, did you hear that?" The lady, annoyed at what she called the vulgarity of the parrot, informed the company that she had a parrot which, although exceedingly clever, was never guilty of coarse language, and who usually addressed visitors with the phrase, "Funny thing! what are you doing there?" The doctor asked the loan of the lady's parrot, that his own might profit by its superior culture, and gaining her consent, dispatched his unwilling butler to fetch the missionary bird. The butler was met with the usual formula, "Funny thing! what are you doing there?" to which he answered roughly: "You ugly brute! I shouldn't have been here but for you!" and taking the cage with him returned to the doctor's house. The lady welcomed her pet with its own words : "Funny thing ! what are you doing there ? " and to her intense disgust was answered in the words of the butler : "You ugly brute ! I shouldn't have been here but for you ?" This was naturally too much for the doctor's parrot, who immediately screamed out : "Great Scott, M'Gregor, did you hear that ?"

Withdrawing.—At a signal from the hostess, the ladies rise and the gentleman nearest to the door opens it, that they may proceed to the withdrawing-room. Cigars and wines and the last new stories are then discussed by the gentlemen, until such time as the host feels that they are due in the drawing-room, when he rises and leads the way. The time spent over dinner—and it is the last thing in the world that should be hurried over—usually leaves but little time for after-amusement, and in the ordinary way the guests depart soon after the ladies have been joined by the gentlemen, unless indeed the dinner has been an especially early one, announced as preceding a reception. A little music, and a little conversation of a more general character than is possible at the dinner table takes place, but after this the guests begin to disperse. Youth should never be the first to leave, unless under pressure, and when taken the departure should be made with the least possible fuss. Every guest should shake hands with the host and hostess before leaving, and call and leave cards within a week after his visit.

GOURMET ET GOURMAND.

Epicurus never taught
Wild excess and wanton sport ;
His to differentiate
Between the coarse and delicate.

Highest good and sweetest pleasure
Follow perfect taste and measure ;
Only theirs who choose the wiser,
O wine-bibbing gormandiser.

Follow Epicurus' suit :
Feed the angel, not the brute.—A. H. M.

AT TABLE.

Hunger is the best sauce.—*Old Saying.*

May good digestion wait on appetite and health on both.—SHAKESPEARE.

To know how to eat well is a third part of wisdom.—*Anon.*

Many dig their graves with their teeth.
—FRANKLIN.

Come, gentlemen, let us drink down all unkindness.—SHAKESPEARE.

Dine with pleasure when you may
Dine with pride another day.—M.

He that is rich need not live sparingly, he that can live sparingly need not be rich.

Be the meat but beans and peas,
God be thanked for those and these.
Have we bread or have we fish,
All are fragments of His dish.
Old Rhyme.

The poor man must walk to get meat for his stomach, the rich man to get stomach for his meat.—FRANKLIN.

Man is a dining animal
Whose wants must be supplied.
Who may not join the cannibal
Must other food abide.
So fish, and fowl, and mammal
He gorges to his taste,
And imitates the camel
In the region of his waist.
And when he's fed till he can eat no more,
His victims join him in a general snore.—A. H. M.

Our life is but a winter's day:
Some only breakfast and away;
Others to dinner stay, and are full fed;
The oldest only sups and goes to bed.
Large is his debt who lingers out the day;
Who goes the soonest has the least to pay.
CORNOCH.

PUBLIC DINNERS

WHATEVER the world may weary of; and men get tired of most things in the course of time, it never seems to lose its appetite for eating and drinking. Individuals may, and do become *blasé*, and were it not for perennial indiscretions in the choice of foods, in the methods of cooking, and in the manner of eating and drinking, the medical profession would soon lose the greater part of its income, and yet, happily for the human race, the vast majority of people maintain those healthy conditions of supply and demand which enable them to " throw physic to the dogs " and to enjoy, without stint or waste, " the kindly fruits of the earth."

The private dinner party has been already dealt with, and it may be said of the public dinner that while it loses to a large extent the intimate social charm of the select dinner table it adds in compensation the inspiration of numbers, and commonly the interest of occasion, some object of special concern being usually the *raison d'être* of the festival. Hospitality is a common virtue of humanity, and it would be profitless to attempt to determine what age or peoples have been most given to its display, but wherever shown, it is universally admitted that the social consumption of good food is a sure promoter of good feeling, and that it is always safer to make claims upon human generosity after, than before a meal. This is true of all time, and operates all the world over. We have a saying that " the way to an Englishman's heart is through his stomach," and Sydney Smith once recommended a colonial bishop to apply this formula to ingratiate himself with his flock by always keeping a nice piece of cold missionary ready on the sideboard, in case a native might call. It is on this principle that public dinners are frequently

2

organised in the cause of charity and for the furtherance of philanthropic enterprises. Lord Beaconsfield once said that he attributed the good feeling maintained in political circles among rival politicians to the Englishman's habit of talking politics after dinner, and this too is a tribute to the humanising and harmonising influence of the social feast.

Public dinners are held for a large variety of purposes—to celebrate anniversaries, to mark public events, to crown great occasions and to honour distinguished men. As most business assemblies model their procedure on the methods of the "Mother of Parliaments," most public dinners follow the precedents of state banquets and the great dinners of the larger public institutions.

The progress of civilisation is said to be marked by developments of refinement in the habits of eating and drinking, and it would be interesting, if space permitted, to compare point by point the characteristics of the ancient and the modern banquet. Pepys lifts the curtain and gives us an interesting peep at the Lord Mayor's feast of 1663, Sir Anthony Bateman's year. He says "At noon I went forth by coach to Guildhall. . . . We went up and down to see the tables where, under every salt there was a bill of fare, and at the end of the table the persons proper for the table. Many were the tables, but none in the hall but the Mayor's and the Lords of the Privy Council that had napkins or knives, which was very strange." It appears that the introduction of the fork, which came from Italy, put the napkin out of countenance for a time, and it is probable that the guests brought a knife and fork with them. "I sat at the merchant strangers' table," continues the diarist ; "where ten good dishes to a messe . . . but it was very unpleasing that we had no napkins nor change of trenchers, and drank out of earthen pitchers and wooden dishes." These banquets are said to have cost from £700 to £800. Accounts show that as late as the year 1782 no fewer than 1,249 bottles of wine were consumed at the Lord Mayor's banquet. Port was the leading temptation in those days, and 438 bottles of suppressed gout were disposed of at this feast, to say nothing of 220 bottles of Lisbon, which is said to have been a wine of similar character. 168 bottles of claret figured in the list, 143 of champagne, 116 of Burgundy, 90 of Madeira, 66 of hock, 4 of malmsey or sack and 4 of brandy. It will be seen by these facts that much progress has been made since Pepys had more or less to " eat with his fingers," and six-bottle men finished their dinners under the table.

Of the dinners themselves little need be said. Menus vary, but they never fail to explain themselves as well, at least, as the chef's knowledge of kitchen French will allow, and the price paid for the ticket is usually some guide as to the variety if not the quality the diner may expect. The writer once insisted upon the menu for a dinner over which he presided being printed in English. He will not repeat the experiment. Bad French may not be appetising, but bad English is positively indigestible.

At public dinners the price of the ticket often includes a first course of wine. This varies, but includes the wine placed on the table in the first instance, and usually carries the diner as far as the entrées, but does not include champagne.

AFTER-DINNER SPEECHES.

After-dinner speeches are much less the order of the day than formerly, but at most public dinners toasts are proposed and spoken to, and those who can speak with ease and grace are always in demand. After-dinner oratory should be as light as the dessert, and as sparkling as the champagne. Dull speeches are a nuisance at any time, but after dinner they are anathema maranatha. In the following pages a number of specimen speeches are given, more by way of suggestion than as models to be committed to memory and delivered word for word. As two or three examples are given in most cases, the speaker who finds it convenient to use such aids will be able to select points from one and another which, linked up with his own thoughts, may be easily adapted to the occasion which demands his effort.

Those who are called upon to respond to the toasts drunk are usually persons in some way associated with the institutions or vocations which the toast is designed to honour, and therefore may reasonably be expected to be familiar with the interests they are called upon to represent. As their main duty is merely to say "Thank you," with as much dignity and grace as they can command, and add perhaps a few words upon points raised in the speech of the proposer, there is no need to supply them with suggestions as to subject-matter. The one caution the specialist needs perhaps more than any other speaker is one against prolixity. Some men cannot resist the temptation to let themselves go on occasion, and when Professor Dry-as-dust sets out to air his pet theories, or Dr. Hum-and-haw insists on riding his time-worn hobbies to death, the result can only be weariness of the flesh and vexation of spirit. Brevity is the soul of wit; and all after-dinner speeches should be short and sweet.

As already indicated, there is a tendency to reduce the number of speeches on public occasions, and where orators are few it is well to do so. Good speaking is always listened to with pleasure and profit, but it is too much to expect any company to drink the health of others at the expense of their own, and long, dull, and heavy speeches are not healthy at any time.

THE TOAST LIST.

The first three toasts, the order of which is invariably followed, are 1. THE KING; 2. THE QUEEN, QUEEN ALEXANDRA, THE PRINCE OF WALES AND THE OTHER MEMBERS OF THE ROYAL FAMILY; and 3. THE IMPERIAL FORCES: THE NAVY, AND THE ARMY. The third toast is usually responded to by representatives of the Admiralty, and the Horse Guards, or by officers of the respective services. The fourth toast at such banquets as those given at the Guildhall on November 9, or by the Royal Academy on the eve of the opening of their annual exhibitions is His Majesty's Ministers. These are both occasions upon which some members of the Cabinet are present, and the duty of responding falls upon the Prime Minister. At the Guildhall Banquet the fifth toast is commonly "Their Excellencies the Foreign Ministers," and the sixth, "The Judges and the Bar of England." These are followed by toasts honouring the outgoing and the incoming Lord Mayors and Sheriffs. At the Royal Academy Banquet of 1911 the same order was followed up to toast four, after which an omnibus toast was proposed by Sir Edward Poynter in terms which will explain the reason, and emphasise observations already made. In proposing the toast of "The Guests," he said: "Of late years it has been what I cannot but regard as a laudable custom, to curtail the number of speeches at public dinners, and we have found it advisable to conform to what is, no doubt, a general wish. We have therefore included in the toast 'The Guests,' the representatives of the various offices of dignity and of such professional pursuits as science, literature, music and the drama; which we formerly distinguished by special toasts." This practice has been largely followed elsewhere, and the example may be commended for adoption to an even wider extent. In this case the names of distinguished members of the professions expected to respond are coupled with the toast, and in the result the speeches are not necessarily fewer, but at least the abandonment of the formal proposal of each one separately saves time, and the pledging of a number of toasts in one is favourable to temperance. Those expected to respond should in all cases be invited to do so, or at least "forewarned," that they may be "forearmed." It is not polite, and it is often unkind, to take speakers by surprise.

MODES OF ADDRESS.

In addressing the company at a banquet, care should be taken to open with a formula which includes all those who are present. At a Guildhall Banquet of November 9 this formula would be: "My Lord Mayor, Your Excellencies, My Lords, Ladies, and Gentlemen; the term "Your Excellencies," being used in reference to Foreign Ministers. Inexperienced speakers are not likely to be called upon to speak first on such occasions, and their best cue as to methods of address is the form followed by earlier speakers.

Young speakers should be careful in these matters, for it is very easy in the confusion of the moment to say Ladies and Gentlemen when there are no ladies present, or to use the word gentlemen only when the audience is a mixed one. The first error always causes a smile, the second often causes annoyance. Speakers unaware what distinguished guests may be present should consult the printed list.

THE LOYAL TOASTS.

The first toast, as we have already seen, is always that of "THE KING." It is proposed by the President, who speaks to it or not at his discretion. As a rule, the less said the better, for no argument is necessary, and the toast is always sure of being drunk with full honours. At the same time, two or three sentences felicitously associating, where possible, the King's known sympathies with the occasion celebrated, or the object and purpose of the gathering held, may well be made. If musical honours are intended, it is just as well to make sure that the pianist is in his place before the National Anthem is announced. Few things are more annoying to the president—who often enough is a man of distinction who ought not to be annoyed—than a hitch in these elementary ceremonial matters due to unreadiness or misunderstanding.

Where strict rule is observed, the toast of "THE QUEEN, QUEEN ALEXANDRA, THE PRINCE OF WALES and the other members of the Royal Family" follows; and here again felicitous references to amiable qualities known to exist are admissible, but obviously all references to Royalty must be made in the best of taste. All the Royal toasts are proposed from the chair, and in the absence of Royalty, are drunk without acknowledgment or response.

Other toasts follow according to the toast list, which varies with the occasion.

The King (*Proposed by the Chairman*).

Ladies and Gentlemen, the first toast given at all gatherings of Englishmen is that of "The King!" It is a toast which carries with it its own passport, and as such requires no argument in its support. To give reasons for it would be to suggest necessity where none exists, and to inflict verbosity where none is needed. Ladies and gentlemen, all upstanding, I give you the toast of toasts, "The King!"

The King (*An Alternative*).

Ladies and Gentlemen, the first toast which I have the honour and pleasure of proposing to you to-night is " A Health unto His Majesty The King ! "

We who are old enough to remember the glories of three reigns, who still look back with loving memory to the long and happy reign of the great and good Queen Victoria ; who yet remember the geniality and grace of the rule of Edward the Peacemaker, and who now contemplate the virtues of the best travelled and most up-to-date monarch in the world, will not need much persuasion to induce us to rise with alacrity and drink with enthusiasm to the perpetuation of a dynasty so rich in the glory of the past, and so full of hope for the future.

Those men are the most successful in common life who best adapt themselves from time to time to the ever-changing conditions of their environment, and England is happy and safe to-day in the hands of a King who looks with twentieth-century eyes upon the modern trend of things, who, by personal experience, knows more of his own dominions than any of his predecessors ever learned, and more of the policy and enterprise of other nations than perhaps any of his royal contemporaries evidence, and whose " Wake up England," uttered at the very heart of Empire on his return from his famous tour, rang like a trumpet peal throughout the length and breadth of the world, loosening the purse-strings of capital, quickening the brain of enterprise, and nerving the arm of labour to the maintenance of our proud pre-eminence in the forefront of the progress of mankind.

Ladies and Gentlemen, I give you the first of loyal toasts, " The King ! His Majesty King George V."

The King (*Another Alternative*).

Ladies and Gentlemen, in these days when party politics merely mark off the different regiments of loyal soldiers who battle for King and country, any one upon whom the duty may fall can rise with perfect confidence and propose the health of the reigning monarch.

Time was when he who dared the loyal purpose did so at some risk—he stood in danger of the headsman's axe, and was shadowed by the dagger of the assassin. In those days the King was pledged with bated breath, and cheered in whispers. Toasts were robed in riddles, and disguised in innuendoes. We all remember the famous toast :

> "God bless the King—I mean the Faith's defender.
> God bless—no harm in blessing—the Pretender.
> Who the Pretender is and who the King,
> God bless us all, that's quite another thing."

Of this spirit was the answer of the noble countess who was reproached for not praying for the King—" For the King," she said, " I do pray ; but I do not think it necessary to tell my God who *is* the King."

In the days when no King was, the same necessity obtained

> "Into the Devil Tavern
> Three booted troopers strode ;
> From spur to feather spotted and splashed
> With the mud of the winter's road ;
> In each of their cups they dropped a crust
> And stared at the guests with a frown ;
> Then drew their swords and roared for a toast,
> ' God send this crum-well down ! ' "

But, Ladies and Gentlemen, we live in happier times ; we meet without a bode of evil, none daring to make us afraid, and, conscious that of all the forms of government the world has ever known, the purest politics and the cleanest administrations prosper under a limited monarchy, we rise with enthusiasm—a mixed assembly with a single aim—differing in many matters, but one in loyalty to the supreme head of the State, and drink this toast to the common good. Ladies and Gentlemen, " The King ! "

The Queen, Queen Alexandra, the Prince of Wales, and the other Members of the Royal Family.

Ladies and Gentlemen, intimately associated with the last toast—as intimately, indeed, as are the distinguished persons the two toasts seek to honour—is the toast I now have the privilege to propose : The Queen, Queen Alexandra, the Prince of Wales, and the other Members of the Royal Family."

Happy as we have been for many years past under a succession of supreme rulers of the State who have magnified their office, and borne with grace and dignity " the fierce light that beats upon the throne," we have been equally favoured under the royal consorts who have shared their responsibilities and honours. Albert the Good, who died all too soon, left a memory and an influence which still survive; Alexandra of Denmark, who conquered England as her forbears never could, still holds her own in the hearts of a loving and admiring people; and the consort of King George V., whom we remember with affection as the Princess May— a name which stands for all that is bright and promising in the springtime of nature and of life, and whom we now honour with enthusiasm as Queen Mary—the sweetest name of all— sustains her noble office in a manner well befitting the best traditions of the past, and fully worthy the imitation of consorts yet to come.

Of the Prince of Wales and the younger members of the Royal Family I need only remind you that they are growing up under the best of home influences, and amid the wisest of educational counsels, and that we have every right to hope that, given the health we now wish them, they will follow the best examples of their ancestors and become the pride of their parents and the honour of their country.

Ladies and Gentlemen, the toast is "The Queen, Queen Alexandra, the Prince of Wales, and the other members of the Royal Family."

The Queen, etc. (*An Alternative.*)

Ladies and Gentlemen, it is among the disabilities of kings that commonly they are not free to marry ladies of their own country, and it is matter of history that they have often been called upon to prejudice, if not to sacrifice, their own domestic felicity in diplomatic exigencies for political gain. The influence of foreign queens upon English policy is a long and romantic story, whose pages are blotted with the people's tears, and reddened with the nation's best blood.

But England to-day is in a happier case, for His Majesty King George V. was fortunate in being free to marry the daughter of an English Princess, who was born a native of the country over which she has been called upon to reign. On her first appearance in society, she expressed a wish to be called Princess Mary of

2*

England, and from that day to this she has been English through and through.

Surely we may congratulate ourselves that at the time of the federation of the hundred Englands up and down the sea, we have, united upon a united throne and ruling over a united people, a King and Queen who are each of them free from foreign prejudices, and who are both animated by the national spirit.

Ladies and Gentlemen, the toast is "Her Majesty the Queen, Queen Alexandra, the Prince of Wales, and the other members of the Royal Family." May they long live to adorn their high positions, and enjoy the love and confidence of a united people.

The Queen, etc. (*Another Alternative*).

Ladies and Gentlemen, much as we honour royalty and admire the great qualities that lend lustre to the throne, it is the domestic virtues which appeal most nearly to English hearts, and for all our admiration for the grace and dignity that invest the court with an atmosphere of awe, it is the human characteristics which affect us most nearly—the "touch of nature which makes the whole world kin," a touch which lifts the monarch above the crown and the woman above the queen.

In Her Majesty Queen Mary we have a lady as up to date as her royal husband. Animated by the modern spirit, she realises that she can best serve the interests of the King by being well informed upon the great questions that demand his serious attention, and with this view, takes care to keep in close touch with European problems and national politics. As a mother, she has aimed at encouraging the spirit of independence among her children, and by teaching them, when young, to wait upon themselves, has given them the best qualifications to direct servants when wider responsibilities involve them in more important duties. Herself proficient in the French and German languages, with which she keeps in practice by constant reading, she is insistent that her children shall acquire equal facility in the mastery of languages, which will in later years keep them *en rapport* with French feeling and German thought. As a housewife, she orders domestic matters with the ease of one familiar with every detail, and as one not disdaining personal service.

A wise queen, a true wife, and a model mother, I give you the toast of " Her Majesty the Queen, of Queen Alexandra of queenly memories, of the Prince of Wales, our future King, and the other members of the Royal Family."

The Imperial Forces. The Navy, the Army.
Proposed by the Chairman or some one appointed.

Ladies and Gentlemen, although we are a peace-loving people, who cherish the hope that time may, and will, come when peaceful methods of conference will supersede " the stern arbitrament of war," we cannot and do not shut our eyes to the fact that in the meantime the best security for peace must be that the balance of power should rest in the hands of those most peaceably disposed. There is no nation on the earth more peaceably disposed than Great Britain, and if our proposition be true, there is no country in the world more fitted to hold the balance of power. Supreme fitness always carries with it paramount obligations, and in the discharge of this duty England is forced to arm in the interests of peace. Gerald Massey sings :

> " For we are peacemen, also, crying for
> Peace, peace at any price, though it be war."

Ladies and Gentlemen, if we organise institutions charged with this grave responsibility, we cannot escape the duty of wishing them good health, and where is the one amongst us who wishes to escape any duty whatsoever ? Proud of their great accomplishments in the historic past, safe in the security of their present protection, and confident in their ability to defend us in the future, I give you the toast " The Army and Navy, and Auxiliary Forces."

The Imperial Forces (*An Alternative*).

Ladies and Gentlemen, John Bull is proud of his Island home, and, small as it is, he would venture all his other wealth in its defence.

Our insular position ensures us great freedom and involves us in some disadvantages. We are free from quarrels over boundaries, and are not harassed by the predatory incursions which are common when lines of demarcation are indistinct. We are no longer subject to raids across our border, for the British Isles are one nation, and for the rest, the armadas of the world are not equal to the conquest of the surrounding seas, which lie like a protecting arm thrown round a united people, to give them their first line of defence.

When we think of the favoured position that we geographically occupy, and the wondrous record we historically hold, we are emboldened, without boasting and with true thankfulness to the Giver of all good, under whose providence we live and prosper, to say with Sir Robert Grant :

> " *Our land*, with its store
> Of wonders untold,
> Almighty, Thy power
> Hath founded of old,
> Hath 'stablished it fast
> By a changeless decree,
> And round it hath cast,
> Like a mantle, the sea."

But besides our first line of defence, we have a second—" the thin red line "—of immortal memory, that has borne the flag of freedom over hill and plain, through jungle fastnesses, and over desert wastes to stay the hand of tyranny and strike the fetters from the slave, and that still exists, clad in a more sober hue, to hold the liberties our fathers won, and to guard the empire upon which the sun never sets.

Ladies and Gentlemen, the toast is " The Imperial Forces, The Navy and the Army."

The Army (*An Alternative*).

Ladies and Gentlemen, the valour of our arms is a thrice-told tale, and the Jingoes, who are for ever bragging of our military pre-eminence, only depreciate the virtues they attempt to extol. The merest suspicion of braggadocio is repugnant to the sense of the heroic. Surely no nation has less need to exaggerate the prowess of its soldiers than the one that can point to a thousand victories, marking the epochs of history and the stepping-stones of civilisation, often won under all but impossible circumstances, and commonly against all but overwhelming odds.

Happily for us, when we are celebrating the valour of our armies, we are not called upon

to justify the policy that has too often given
them employment. The motive of a war may
be without defence, but there is always glory
at the cannon's mouth.

The statesman who plays with human lives
as a savant plays at chess, may crown a great
ambition with a splendour that hides a greater
shame, but no man, however humble, ever bared
his bosom, at the call of duty, to the bullets
of the enemy in a quarrel which was not his own,
but proved himself to be of imperishable metal
cast in true heroic mould.

Nothing can justify the campaign of wanton
plunder led by the Black Prince in 1356, but
quite as truly it may be said that no words are
equal to the sum of heroism which led his little
band of Englishmen to dare the chances of
Poitiers, and face, defy, and then defeat at odds
of ten to one, the chosen chivalry of France.

Ladies and Gentlemen, here's to our Imperial
Forces, officers and men—"The Army."

The Navy (*An Alternative*).

Ladies and Gentlemen, from the earliest
ages England has recognised as its first ally
the ocean that rolls round about her coasts. A
thousand years ago the great father of our
history, Alfred the Great, founded the policy
of meeting the enemies of our country upon the
sea, and in this demonstrated the fact that
there are occasions when it may become worth
while to meet trouble half-way. To render
that policy effective he built a Navy to defend
the land against invasion, and from that day to
this, while arms have changed and methods
have been altered, while the arrow has given
place to the bullet, and the iron plate has
superseded the wooden wall, the same policy
has been pursued, and all the world has had
the benefit of the freedom of the seas while
Britannia ruled the waves.

Our naval history has been one long epic,
full of heroism and romance; and though the
age of iron has not sustained the old romance
which ever lingers round the story of our wooden
walls, with their freer opportunities for the
display of personal prowess, and their larger
incentives to individual daring, and although
we do fight our battles upon sea and land with

machines as much as men, there was never a time in all our history when greater pluck was needed by those who protect us from the enemy and the destroyer. The miner shows his bravery when he runs the risk of fire-damp and living burial, that he may dig the coal to speed the engines of the world, but what of the miner who works in the hold of the ironclad to feed her giant engines with that selfsame coal, without a chance to save himself should the hull be rammed? It is one thing to fight hand-to-hand with fair exchange of chances, but quite another thing to drop dead at a mile, and never see the hand that sped the blow. And yet we do not fail us of our brave defenders, and we shall all be ready to add appreciative encouragement, and join in Gerald Massey's manly appeal:

> "Come, show your colours now, my lads,
>   That all the world may know
> The boys are equal to their dads
>   Whatever blasts may blow.
>
> "All hands aboard, our country calls
>   On her seafaring folk;
> In giving up our wooden walls
>   More need of hearts of oak."

Full of gratitude for the triumphs of the past, full of confidence in the courage of the future, we will strike another stanza of the poet's song:

> "Old England still throbs with the muffled fire
>   Of a past she can never forget,
> And again shall she herald the world up higher:
>   There's life in the old land yet."

Ladies and Gentlemen, "The Imperial Forces, The Navy."

His Majesty's Ministers.

Ladies and Gentlemen, the toast I have the honour to propose is that of "His Majesty's Ministers."

To whatever school of political thought we may belong, and whatever party organisation we may generally support, we are all sensible enough to appreciate the other side of argument, and generous enough to recognise the merits of opponents.

Party divisions are very much the result of temperament, and political controversy is often a struggle between thoughts and feelings. Both are factors in national life, and there are times when each has its part to play in determining national policy.

Under a constitution like ours, where His Majesty's Ministers are chosen by the joint will of the people and the King, the Government for the time being is usually the best that can be, pending an appeal to the electorate for further orders ; and however much we may differ from the men chosen on issues large or small, we are all under great obligation to them for the enormous responsibilities they bear, and for the splendid ability they devote to what they believe to be the best interests of us all.

Ladies and Gentlemen, health is a prime necessity of all good work, and even though we may differ from the Cabinet from time to time, since their best work is, for the time being, the best work that can be, it becomes us all to drink with heartiness, if not enthusiasm, " The Health of His Majesty's Ministers."

The Houses of Parliament.

Ladies and Gentlemen, among the many institutions of which Great Britain is justly proud, there are few that can be said to rank in national esteem with the Houses of Parliament.

As a nation we pride ourselves upon the integrity of our justice and our love of fair play ; upon the soundness of our finance and the honesty of our industrial methods ; upon the sincerity of our political aims, and the reality of our patriotic devotion ; and finding all these qualities operative in our legislature, we recognise them as reflections of our national character, and are really paying an incidental compliment to ourselves when for these reasons we give " honour to whom honour is due."

Of course we do not waive our constitutional right of grumbling at Parliaments, as well as at everything else ; and sometimes their contentions are so provoking that we are inclined to cry out, " A plague on both your houses," and sigh for some drastic method of compelling them to employ their common sense for the common good. For one half of John Bull's happy family they are generally far too slow, for the other half they are always much too dangerously fast, and yet, notwithstanding these defects, we are all proud to regard our Parliament as the safest, surest, and most business-like legislative assembly in the world.

We hear much in our day of revolutions, and history has many an instructive page upon the subject. But revolutions may be constructive or destructive, and monuments of the one and ruins of the other lie all along the paths of progress. Happily for us, under our constitution, constructive revolutions can take place with no more disturbance of the national peace than follows the revolutions of the world as it rolls round the sun and leads all its children in turn from darkness to light.

Ladies and Gentlemen, I give you " The Houses of Parliament."

The Bench and Bar.

Ladies and Gentlemen, it has been said that a legal career offers the shortest road to the highest honours of the country. Given the endowment of necessary natural gifts, and an equal measure of physical health and industrial application, a barrister has a better chance of reaching the woolsack in the House of Lords than the curate has of occupying the throne of an archbishop, and the subaltern of wielding the baton of a field-marshal.

If this is so, perhaps it is the reason why the law attracts to its practice so large a number of the most brilliant of Britain's gifted sons. But whether for this reason, or for some other, certain it is that the Bench and Bar of England display an intellectual strength, a forensic skill, and a scrupulous honesty of which all the Englands are proud. Some people are fond of attributing the pre-eminence of our country among the nations of the earth to our military power, our naval supremacy, our diplomatic skill, and our genius for colonisation ; and no doubt all these play a great part in our influence upon the world ; but in and through these, as well as apart from them, the strong hold we have upon the honour of other nations is the integrity of our justice, the soundness of our finance which grows out of it, and the honesty of our trade which follows.

Strong as this appeal is to the larger nations

of the earth, it has an even more powerful effect upon smaller and less civilised communities. Our humbler fellow-subjects in the remoter parts of the world know full well that English justice is not bought or sold, and that, as a rule, when they submit a case to an English tribunal they do so without fear or favour, and with every confidence of obtaining equal justice. They know too that they will not be punished more than once for one offence, and they will not be called upon to pay the same taxes twice over.

This we owe to the spirit of justice and the love of fair play, which is an integral part of the English character, and which finds its active expression in Bench and Bar.

Ladies and Gentlemen, malice has sometimes suggested that indigestion is often more powerful than evidence in influencing judgment, but without for a moment admitting so foul a calumny, we shall all agree that whether we are plaintiffs or defendants we are all of us vitally interested in the health of Bench and Bar.

The Medical Profession.

Ladies and Gentlemen, there is no body of men to whom we resign ourselves more unreservedly than to the members of the medical profession. We dispute with our clergy, we argue with our lawyers, and we can always improve upon the designs of our architects; we criticise our artists and actors, and we quarrel roundly with our statesmen and administrators, but we become less dogmatic when we enter the domain of science, and, as a rule, observe passive obedience, as even the doctors themselves do when needing medical attendance. How much of this is due to our confidence in the profession and how much to our want of confidence in ourselves, would perhaps be difficult to decide; but we all recognise the wisdom of the formula, "It is no use consulting a doctor unless you follow his advice," and the measure of our obedience to medical orders is doubtless largely determined by the measure of the weakness that calls for them.

Ladies and Gentleman, as a rule our confidence is not misplaced. There is probably no body of men more uniformly patient, gentle, courteous, and humane and skilful; and often enough the personnel of the doctor is a prime factor in the cures that he effects. No men are more ready at call, more devoted in service, and more ill-requited for labour than the men of the medical profession. There are no men who do more for nothing, and who suffer more from failure and inadequacy of payment.

To the larger triumphs of the medical profession and the progress of sanitary science it is impossible now to refer at length, but it is sufficient for our present purpose to point out that even within modern memory they have largely reduced the tale of human suffering, and they have added to the average length of human life.

Ladies and Gentlemen, while we owe to them our greater health and increased longevity, we shall need no urging to induce us to wish for them the full enjoyment of the fruits of their own labours. I give you the toast of "The Medical Profession."

The Drama.

Ladies and Gentlemen, "All the world's a stage," so Shakespeare says, "and all the men and women merely players"; and whether we follow the drama of life in the world at large, through the pleasant pages of a novel, or amid the picturesque accessories of the stage, we all admit it a profoundly interesting study.

Pope says, "The proper study of mankind is man," and if this be so we have not far to go to school. In the world at large the play is too complex to be comprehended as a whole, and often too bewildering to be understood in parts. In the novel we see the problem at nearer range and focused with clearer definition; but a book makes strong claims upon our patience, and puts no little tax upon our time. On the stage we have the concentration of the vital elements of the drama, without verbosity and studied delay, and we have it presented to us with a vividness which is impossible to the mere word-painter, and a reality of action and emotion which only the human form and voice can reproduce.

In Hamlet s view the office of the play is "to hold as 'twere the mirror up to nature; to show virtue her own features, scorn her own image, and the very age and body of the time his form and pressure"; and this office it has sustained from age to age. As such it has reflected the evil and the good. As the standards of society have fluctuated the drama has reflected their rise and fall, disclaiming all responsibility for aught but the accuracy of the presentation, and so it continues "to show virtue her own features" and "scorn her own image," it will yet serve and chronicle its day and generation, from time to time, and he would be unwise who, esteeming some things evil, would ring down the curtain upon all, as he would be a fool who broke a mirror because it sometimes reflected an ugly truth.

Ladies and Gentlemen, as the health of the stage reflects the health of the times, I am giving you a double toast when I ask you to drink the health of the Drama.

Science.

Ladies and Gentlemen, we live in a scientific age. Some people call it an age of materialism, but whether we are materialists or spiritualists, we are all beggared of wonderment when we contemplate the marvels of modern science.

Within the memory of men still living, the steam engine has minimised distance and linked together the scattered abodes of men— stirring the pulses of humanity and quickening the energies of the world. But a few years ater the electric telegraph flashed new opportunities across the spheres and harnessed the lightning in the service of mankind.

> "On the back of a word a-ride a wire,
> Unseen, unheard, with a heart of fire
> We speed the message of our desire."

Then followed the thousand-and-one applications of electricity to the needs and industries of man:

> "The stars light up the household sky,
> And a million moons rush out on high,
> To light the people passing by.
>
> "The wheels, awhirl with right goodwill,
> Weave the web of the fabric still,
> And grind the grist that comes to the mill."

And then its application to traffic:

> " We turn a handle and off we go,
> And move in a groove in the ground below,
> And thread the traffic to and fro,
> Or trail a-rail, or fast or slow.

> " We burrow and furrow like human moles,
> A-cube in a tube till we reach our goals.

> " We mock the paddle and scorn the sail,
> And stem the tempest and ride the gale."

And then later came the wonder of all electric wonders—the wireless telegraphy, which places on speaking terms the ships that pass in the night, that brings into touch the four corners of the earth, that makes us masters of the empyrean, and may one day bring us into fellowship with the stars.

> " I am the spirit, Thought. In the clumsy garb men praise
> As a thing of sense and sound and sight I walked their common ways.
> Then over their iron threads I paced with patient care.
> But they've found at last, these sons of men, they may trust me to the air.

> " Tell me whither to go. Clothe me and set me free.
> I pass and my winged feet skim the waves of the wide electric sea.
> Where you would have me tarry, make me a welcome there.
> Faithful to you, O sons of men, you may trust me to the air.

> " Freer at last am I to fly as a spirit may,
> With only the weight of the wings I wave. Oh, this foretells the day
> When without speech or language some cunning mind may dare
> Waft me to other minds and know he may trust me to the air."—*Charles P. Cleaves.*

Ladies and Gentlemen, I give you the toast of "Science."

Science (*An Alternative*).

Ladies and Gentlemen, the toast I have the honour to propose is that of Science, and, learned or unlearned, we cannot escape our obligations to do it honour.

Science is systematised truth, and art is truth idealised, and all good purposes are served when truth is demonstrated and beauty worshipped. We investigate natural phenomena, we discover apparently isolated facts; we trace their relationship to one another, and find them grouped in systems; we mark the laws that regulate them, and note their influence upon other systems, and then we give them the names by which they are known—astronomy, geology, mineralogy and metallurgy, and other 'urgies, and 'ologies galore. We invent instruments to bring us into closer touch with our studies. The telescope brings far things near. The microscope makes small things large. The microphone magnifies sound, the telephone speeds it, and the phonograph records it and makes even dead men speak. And so science accumulates knowledge and places it at the disposal of mankind.

Perhaps no department of science makes a more direct appeal to us all than that which devotes itself to the promotion of health. On this subject whole libraries have been written. The discovery of anæsthetics has brought all pain within the area of endurance. The application of the Röntgen rays has enabled skilled observation to locate disease. The power of radium has yet to be demonstrated. And the end is not yet. As Charles Mackay sings:

> "Lo, the world is rich in blessings :
>   Earth and ocean, flame and wind,
>   Have unnumbered secrets still,
>   To be ransacked when you will,
>   For the service of mankind.
>
> "Science is a child as yet,
>   And her power and scope shall grow,
>   And her triumphs in the future
>   Shall diminish toil and woe ;
>   Shall extend the bounds of pleasure,
>   With an ever-widening ken,
>   And of woods and wildernesses
>   Make the homes of happy men."

Ladies and Gentlemen, Science has already so extended boundaries and quickened movements, that it has outstripped our possibility of doing justice to itself. I give you the toast of "Science."

Art.

Ladies and Gentlemen, the toast I have the honour to propose is that of "Art," and in doing so I would first observe that the word art is one of the best abused words in the English language. Even when used by practised speakers, it is often applied indifferently to signify the means whereby we attain artistic ideals, and the finished product itself. Like poetry, art is difficult, if not impossible of definition. As a means to an end, we associate it with the word " crafts," and recognise it as the skilled use of mechanical means to achieve a more than mechanical result. As the end itself, we use it to indicate that more than material result which marks the difference between the work of the mechanic and the artist. All art is an effort after expression, and it employs every available means. The emotions find their ideal expression in poetry, and poetry appeals to the human mind through all the senses. Poetry is the mother of all the arts. It is poetry that clothes the marble limbs with more than marble beauty; poetry that transfigures colour with a light beyond its own ; poetry that inspires tone, and gives to music the blood of life and the wings of worship.

Ladies and Gentlemen, I give you the toast of Art !

Art (*An Alternative*).

Ladies and Gentlemen, we have only to look through some of the early volumes of our illustrated papers to see how immeasurably taste has improved in the last fifty years, and we have only to look at the decoration of our own homes to realise the progress of refinement effected in almost every object of domestic use. Works of art in themselves are more numerous than formerly, and if we have fewer examples of great art, we have a higher standard of average, and a larger field of application : a sense of appreciation of art is infinitely more widespread than formerly.

Art is said to be one of the last acquirements of a luxurious age, and to be a sure precursor of national decay. If this be so, the progress of art might be regarded as a bad omen, but at present, at least, we have no reason to fear. There are many stages of further development which may be safely passed without any fear of Imperial dissolution.

For all their extravagances of excess, the most outrageous fashions of dress in our day will compare very favourably with the costumes in which our great-grandmothers took so much delight, while in the grouping of colours and the designs of ornament there are in wall-papers and in metal-work, as well as furniture, improvements as striking as they are new, not the least happy of the characteristics of which are the preservation of the best traditions of the past in forms better adapted to modern requirements.

Ladies and Gentlemen, whatever may be the state of art at any time, those who look upon it as truth idealised must ever wish it well, assured that while art remains well and healthy, it can have no part in national decay.

Literature.

Ladies and Gentlemen, in proposing the toast of Literature, an Englishman in our time may well claim pride of place. Homer held it for the ancient Greeks, Virgil and Horace for the Augustine age of Roman letters. Dante, Petrarch, and Boccaccio stand for the classical revival of a more modern Italy, and Chaucer, whom Dryden called "the father of English poetry," and who was born when Boccaccio was a young man, started that long line of illustrious poets, the glory of all literature, of whom the greatest were Spenser, Shakespeare, and Milton of the elder time, Pope, Cowper, and Burns of the eighteenth century, and Wordsworth, Coleridge, Scott, Byron, Shelley, and Keats, who heralded the advent of the nineteenth century, an age as full of singers as are the woods in spring.

In the world of Music Germany may claim easy pre-eminence, and boast behind it a noble literature as characteristic of its national genius ; in the world of Art the imagination of *la belle France*, in all that is the outcome of the artistic temperament, from the cartoons on the walls of the Louvre to the meanest objects of common use, excite the admiration, if not the envy of the world ; but in the appreciation of all of these England and the English-speaking nations admit no superiors, even among the children of the masters of colour, form, and sound, nor have they reason to complain of any want of appreciation on the part of other nations of that splendid Literature which is so peculiarly their own.

Ladies and Gentlemen, I give you the toast of this splendid heritage, "Literature."

Literature (*An Alternative*).

Ladies and Gentlemen, there are some people who think that the time has come when literature may be safely removed from the toast list, and that " science " may more usefully and fittingly occupy its place. This of course is an indication of the materialistic tendencies of the times. But, as you know, there is a saying which affirms that " second thoughts are best," and I feel sure that if those who entertain this idea were to give it sufficient thought, they would be forced to the conviction that so long as science has anything to say, literature will have a vocation, and science will be greatly dependent upon it.

What should we know of the science of the past but for the literature that has preserved it ? Of what use would be the science of the present apart from the literature that diffuses it ? And when the whole tale of science has been told, where are we to look for the story of its growth, for the understanding of its application, and for the results of its achievement, except in the literature which perpetuates it ?

No, Ladies and Gentlemen, literature has the first and the last word. We begin by learning our A B C, if we finish by signing our F.R.S. It is with the growth of literature that nations grow, and by the means of literature that the thoughts, discourses, and prophecies of one generation are handed on to the next, for instruction, improvement, and realisation in the ultimate consummation of all knowledge. If it is not in literature to serve science, how is it that the poet can transfigure the dry-as-dust of the doctrinaire into " a thing of beauty " and " a joy for ever " ?

But, Ladies and Gentlemen, Literature has a value of its own, for which we cherish it, and now for its own sake, as well as for the sake of science, which is apt to undervalue it, I give you the toast of Literature.

The Ladies (*Proposed by a Bachelor.*)

Gentlemen, the practice which relegates the toast of the ladies to the youngest bachelor present is a relic of the days of chivalry, and its object is to enable the one who most needs the opportunity to prove himself a worthy champion of the dames, by displaying the ability, and the bravery that deserve the fair. Gentlemen, it requires no great courage to champion

the cause of woman in a gallant assembly like
this, and my fear is not that I may fail to convince you of the worthiness of the toast, but
that I may be unable to demonstrate the sufficiency of the advocate. My confidence lies in
the assurance that you are all of you as enthusi-
astic as I am in the cause for which I speak,
and that, however faltering my accents may be,
the ladies are as safe in your hearts as are the
fixed stars in heaven. In these circumstances
they have no need of further words of mine.
Gentlemen, I give you the toast :

> " Here's to the girl whose eyes are blue,
> Whose heart is fond, whose love is true.
> Here's to the girl whose eyes are brown,
> Too true to shrink, too kind to frown.
> Here's to the girl with eyes of grey,
> Whose smile can drive dull care away.
> Here's to them all of every hue—
> The black, the grey, the brown, the blue."

In brief, Gentlemen—The Ladies.

The Ladies (*Proposed by a Benedict*).

The toast I have the honour to propose is
that of " Woman, lovely woman," and, although
I am aware that man is still liable, as were the
nobility and gentry of the Cannibal Islands,
to burn his fingers when attempting to toast
a woman without a fork, I have the courage of
my convictions, and shall not shrink from the
fiery ordeal.

Gentlemen, woman as an individual never
grows old, but as a body she forms one of the
oldest institutions on record. Not the oldest, of
course, for man was here before her. She gave
him but little start, however, and but short time
to enjoy the felicities of single blessedness.
She was soon after him, and she has been after
him ever since.

It has been said by some " mere man " that,
made from a human rib, woman was nothing
but a side issue from the first, and it has been
added by some lovely woman, that if man really
lost a rib at her birth, he has more than made
up for it, by putting on side ever since. Com-
paring the lot of Adam with that of his myriad
sons, I am inclined to think that Adam had the
best of it. He lost a rib, it is true, but think of
the millions since his time, the thousands in the
world to-day, the number in this room to-night

who, having one less rib to protect it with, have
lost their hearts. Think of the billions who
from first to last, dazzled by the eyes of beauty,
have tripped over the skirts of grace, and lost
at once their balance and their heads. Think
again of that unnumbered host who, in the dark
ages now happily long since passed away, were
even known to lose their tempers, and I am
sure that you will agree with me that Adam's
loss was nothing compared with that of his innumerable heritors.

But, gentlemen, one of the first lessons that a
wise man learns when graduating at the school
of experience is that of the necessity and the
duty of making the best of things. Of course
no one would be so ungallant as to speak of a
woman as a thing; but the sex which is the
most powerful factor in the life of man is one of
those entities of which it is certainly wise, as
well as necessary, to make the best. There are
compensations in all conditions of existence,
and even married life has its ameliorations. As
Sir Walter Scott says :

> " O woman, in our hours of ease
>   Uncertain, coy, and hard to please,
>   And variable as the shade
>   By the light quivering aspen made ;
>   When pain and anguish wring the brow
>   A ministering angel thou ! "

Gentlemen, we must take the fat with the
lean. Of course you will understand that I am
not applying this metaphor to the ladies, but to
the circumstances of life : we must take the
worse with the better, the poorer with the
richer, and the sickness with the health.

Some one has said a man marries three times,
first for love, second for money, and third for a
nurse, and the proverb has it that "variety is
the charm of life."

Happy is the man who finds in one only, and
only one, the love that outlasts every trial, the
wealth that for ever gains in spending, and the
grace and sympathy that soften the couch of
pain, and can even throw a cheering light across
" the valley of the shadow of death."

The Ladies (*Proposed by a Bohemian*).

An old toast and a good toast, and one which
may well be revived to night, is the sparkling
toast, "Women and Wine." By whatever name

the toast of "The Ladies" is labelled, it means
women and wine, for while " Women " is the
subject, wine is the means employed in doing
her honour. The toteetler may of course sing
with rare Ben Jonson :

> " Drink to me only with thine eyes,
>   And I will pledge with mine,
> Or leave a kiss within the cup,
>   And I'll not ask for wine ;"

but such a troubadour will be one so intoxicated
with the beauty of his inamorata that he fails
to appreciate anything else, or one so new to the
felicities of love that, never having experienced
disillusion, he lives in a paradise of fools.

And yet a paradise of fools is a paradise after
all, and for all we know, may last as long in
modern experience and be as real as the one of
old time that sheltered the first lovers of our
race. Why, then, break the spell ?

> "Where ignorance is bliss 'tis folly to be wise."

and were we to convert him, he would only
change his note :

> " If all your beauties one by one,
>   I pledge dear—I am thinking
> Before the list were well begun,
>   I should be dead with drinking."

But lovesick swains are not the only fools.
Extremes meet :

> " He is a fool who thinks by force or skill
>   To turn the current of a woman's will." (SIR S. TUKE.)

> " For if she will she will, you may depend on't,
>   And if she won't, she won't, and there's an end on't."

Tom Moore says :

> " Disguise the bondage as we will,
>   'Tis woman, woman rules us still ;"

and John Dryden adds with immeasurable
common sense :

> " As for the women, though we scorn and flout them,
>   We may live with, but cannot live without them."

If we have the temerity to scorn and flout
them, surely we shall deserve the retribution of
which Congreve warns us :

> "Heaven has no rage like love to hatred turned,
>   Nor hell a fury like a woman scorned."

The union of Women and Wine in this toast

is justified on a logical basis by an unknown
poet in the significant lines :

> "God made man
> Frail as a bubble ;
> God made love,
> Love made trouble.
>
> "God made the vine :
> Was it a sin
> That man made wine
> To drown trouble in ? "

Gentlemen, if this be a true statement of cause
and effect, I give you the bane and the antidote
together, and the moral or immoral of the toast
is this : may the women have enough influence
over us to keep us sober, and the wine enough
solace to make us independent of their caprice.

The Ladies (*Proposed by Paterfamilias*).

Gentlemen, however excellent the reasons
may be for the practice of relegating the toast
of the ladies to the youngest bachelor present,
there is at any rate a great deal to be said in
favour of placing the duty in the hands of
experience, for who is more likely to do full
justice to a toast like this than he who has
had experiences of the sex in her fourfold
relationship of mother, sister, wife, and daughter ?
This is a comprehensive toast, both in its subject
and its appeal, for it is one of those absolute
certainties of life about which there can never
be any dispute, that wherever you find a man,
you can be quite sure that he had a mother.
Here at least I have a perfect basis of appeal,
and a sufficient one, and were it not that I have
to include others, I would close at once by
saying :

> This the toast before all others,
> All upstanding, Boys, " Your mothers."

Of a lesser, and yet still a large number, it is
safe to assume that they have not passed through
the earlier years of life without experiencing
a sister's sweet and servicable influence. Our
most jealous friends, our most candid critics,
our most sincere well-wishers, the measure of
our brotherly indebtedness is beyond estimate.
Those who have no sisters of their own have
sometimes sisters who have proffered that
relationship as compensation for refusing a
nearer and a dearer one ; and others again, more

fortunate in wooing, have found in other people's sisters the opportunity of securing the sweetest of all human associations in the relationship of man and wife. Happy the man who in this union secures a woman who has

> A smile for every joy,
> A tear for every sorrow,
> A consolation for every grief,
> An excuse for every fault,
> A prayer for every misfortune, and
> An encouragement for every hope.

Wordsworth has described her in verse too long for full quotation :

> "She was a phantom of delight,
>   When first she gleamed upon my sight;
>   A lovely apparition, sent
>   To be a moment's ornament.

> "I saw her upon nearer view,
>   A spirit, yet a woman too!
>   Her household motions light and free,
>   And steps of virgin liberty.

> "A creature not too bright and good
>   For human nature's daily food;
>   For transient sorrows, simple wiles,
>   Praise, blame, love, kisses, tears, and smiles.

> "And now I see with eyes serene,
>   The very pulse of the machine;
>   A being breathing thoughtful breath,
>   A traveller between life and death.

> "A perfect woman nobly planned,
>   To warn, to comfort, and command;
>   And yet a spirit still, and bright,
>   With something of angelic light."

No one but a father can appreciate a father's pride in his son's success, or his joy in his daughter's filial regard. And the joy is an imperishable one. The proverb says :

> "My son's my son till he gets him a wife,
>   But my daughter's my daughter all her life;"

and the proverb is true. For all these reasons I propose to you this comprehensive toast, which includes in one sentence of two words our mothers, sisters, wives, and daughters—"The Ladies."

The Ladies (*Proposed by whomsoever will*).

Gentlemen, the toast I have the honour to propose is one that is usually merged in the larger toast, that includes the whole of the gentler sex, and that, being so included, loses the individuality which to-night I invite you to honour. Gentlemen, the toast is :

> "Our unappropriated blessings."

The world is so rich in blessings, that an infinite number of them fail of appreciation. Enough, in all things, is said to be as good as a feast, and where sufficiency obtains superfluity languishes in disregard. As the poet Gray in his incomparable Elegy puts it :

> "Full many a gem of purest ray serene,
>   The dark, unfathomed caves of ocean bear ;
> Full many a flower is born to blush unseen,
>   And waste its sweetness on the desert air."

But it is not only in distant places that wealth and beauty fail of worthy appreciation. In every gathering of men and women the gems are too numerous for individual recognition, and even in a homely garden there are more flowers than can be plucked and worn upon the breast of love. These are the unappropriated blessings which, lacking the distinction of individual selection, I invite you to toast to-night.

First among these let me name " our maiden aunts." Who amongst us who has enjoyed the benefits of this relationship can total the sum of its beneficences ? We can most of us remember in the days of our childhood, a mother's justice, which was associated with more than a mother's mercy, and for which latter we were indebted to maiden aunts. Few of us have forgotten the friendly hand which helped us out of early troubles, and the all-too-slender purse, generously depleted to recruit our own. The sugar-plums of childhood, the cigarettes of youth, the birthday presents out of all proportion to the donor's means and our own deserts. Those of us who are happy husbands and fathers know the advantages our children enjoy from this relationship, and the comforts we experience from the kindly offices of those mothers' helps, whose attentions are not regulated by bonds of servitude, and in whose hands our interests are as safe as in our own. Of course there are Aunt Tabithas, who are the terror of little girls and the monitors of big ones; but even these must be honoured for their sincerity, and may be trusted for their goodwill. Besides these, there are the ladies of the Red Cross and the nurses in our hospitals, and all those who, without the recompense of wedded companionship, smooth the way of life and ease the bed of pain. Gentlemen, in our own interests we must wish them health, and in their own we shall not withhold the pledge of happiness. We drink to the health and happiness of all spinsters. "Our unappropriated blessings."

The Ladies (*Musical Honours*).

Here's to the maiden of bashful fifteen,
    Here's to the widow of fifty;
Here's to the flaunting extravagant quean,
    And here's to the wife that is thrifty.
Let the toast pass, drink to the lass,
I'll warrant she'll prove an excuse for a glass.

"Here's to the charmer whose dimples we prize,
    Here's to the maid who has none, sir;
Here's to the girl with a pair of blue eyes,
    And here's to the nymph with but one, sir.
Let the toast pass, drink to the lass,
I'll warrant she'll prove an excuse for a glass.

"Here's to the maid with a bosom of snow,
    Here's to her that's as brown as a berry;
Here's to the wife with a face full of woe,
    And here's to the girl that is merry.
Let the toast pass, drink to the lass,
I'll warrant she'll prove an excuse for a glass.

"For let 'em be clumsy, or let 'em be thin,—
    Young or ancient, I care not a feather;
Come fill up the bumper quite up to the brim,
    And let us e'en toast them together.
Let the toast pass, drink to the lass,
I'll warrant she'll prove an excuse for a glass."

AT A WEDDING—The Bride and Bridegroom.

Ladies and Gentlemen, a very simple and pleasing duty devolves upon us all to-day. It is that of joining together to wish health and happiness to those whose nuptials we have met to celebrate.

There are many important days in the lives of men and women. The day of birth is an important day, though we rarely realise it at the time. The day we begin school is an important day, though we seldom recognise it until our school-days are over. The day of our majority is an important day, and one we do not usually undervalue; but there is no day in a life's career which can for a moment compare in importance with the wedding day.

In some sense it is a day of days, including the characteristics of all these other days. It is the birthday, as a rule, of a new household, it is certainly the starting of a new curriculum in the school of life, and it is the attainment of that maturity in human responsibility which is the basis of civic unity, national integrity, and imperial power.

If we were asked to name the institution which lies nearest to the foundations of our national greatness, I doubt if we could give a better answer than to name the institution of marriage.

"Be it ever so humble, there's no place like home," and it is the homes of England, far more than "the towers along her steeps," which make us jealous for the peace of the world and strong for national defence. Hence the building of a home is more important than the building of a Dreadnought. Arms become obsolete and machines get out of date, but Home is a universal and an everlasting word, which includes both Earth and Heaven.

Ladies and Gentlemen, it is the laying of the foundation of an English home that gives us festival to-day; and I am persuaded that where mutual respect lays these foundations, where mutual affection is the contractor, where mutual sympathy is the architect, and mutual forbearance the builder, there must ever rise one of those temples of domestic peace which are the power of an empire's being and the strength of a nation's life. Ladies and Gentlemen, I give you "The Bride and Bridegroom."

The Bride and Bridegroom (*An Alternative*).

Ladies and Gentlemen, it is not always that pleasure and duty go hand in hand, and it is sometimes an unhappy thing for our convenience that we are called upon to choose betwixt the two. But however this may operate in ordinary cases, it certainly presents me with no difficulty now, for I know of no duty more pleasurable and no pleasure more dutiful than that which calls me to my feet, which is to ask you to join with me in wishing health, happiness, and prosperity to the Bride and Bridegroom. It is a pleasure with enough of duty in it to give it zest, a duty with enough of pleasure in it to make it sweet. Many and various are the occasions upon which we meet together to promote business or pleasure, and a large number of these are represented in our gathering to-day. There are political meetings, for instance, rib-boned and badged in the interest of every conceivable political party; and all these parties are represented here.

It is a Unionist meeting for instance, and we are all uniting to bless a union of loyal hearts. It is a Home Rule meeting too, and it is not often that two such meetings are held beneath the same roof, and at the same time. Then it is a Liberal meeting in the thoughts and sentiments it calls forth, and the gifts for which it gives such good occasion, and Radical in the changes it will effect in the lives of those we honour with our toast; and finally, it is Conservative of one of the oldest and best institutions which make for the happiness of all. Then it is a garden party —another Eden, with our up-to-date Adam and a modern Eve, and a horticultural show in which the ladies blossom as the rose, and the gentlemen flourish like the green bay-tree; and when we gaze upon the rich array of presents that the love of friends has outspread with such lavish hands, who will say it does not resemble a grand bazaar? And now, with all the loyalty and earnestness which animate these many and various gatherings, I ask you to join with me in drinking to the loyal union of the happy couple, to the perfect harmony of their home rule, to their liberal enjoyment of all material benefits, and to the conservation of all that is true and good in the traditions of domestic life. Ladies and Gentlemen, I give you "The Bride and Bridegroom."

The Bridegroom's Response.

Ladies and Gentlemen, my first, and perhaps my only duty on this occasion, is on behalf of my wife and myself to thank the proposer of the toast for all the kind, good, and witty things he said in proposing it, and you for the heartiness and goodwill with which you joined in its support.

There are few more embarrassing positions a man can occupy than that which falls to my lot to-day. There are some, I admit, almost as embarrassing, which anticipate the greater embarrassment that now is. There is often no little embarrassment in making the first proposal, which starts the train of carriages which carry us to marriage junction; but this usually takes place in private, and there are frequently, on such occasions, little encouragements which materially alleviate embarrassment, and remove the necessity for speech. Ladies and Gentlemen, you may take it from me as a matter of experience, that there are times when speech is quite superfluous and lips can be far more eloquent and convincing when otherwise engaged. There is some embarrassment often in facing parental dignity; but this again is a private meeting, and even when unsatisfactory to the interviewer there is commonly no impediment to rapid retreat. "None but the brave deserve the fair," and men should always be ready to *face* difficulties in the cause of love. An irate father is just one of those difficulties upon which it is not wise to turn one's back.

But, Ladies and Gentlemen, neither of these embarrassments is with me now, and my one trouble is that I can neither express my own feelings, nor those of my wife, on this happy consummation of our hopes, nor adequately acknowledge your kind and generous wishes for our future well-being. And yet in your good wishes I find all the encouragement I need. You who wish us well with such sincerity will not be too critical of my maiden speech, and will, I am sure, make up out of the fullness of your own generosity for all its numerous shortcomings. Ladies and Gentlemen, in this confidence, on my wife's behalf, and on my own, I say—I thank you.

The Bridesmaids

Ladies and Gentlemen, a wedding is much too serious a matter to be made light of, and far be it from me to introduce levity upon so solemn an occasion. It used to be said that everybody cried at weddings, and all for different reasons. The bride cried because she was being married, and the bridesmaids cried because they were not. The mothers cried because when a *wench* left home there was always a *wrench* in home associations, and when bachelors set up in business for themselves, or retired into private life—whichever you like to call it—there were always batches of old-time recollections, which, welling up from the cisterns of memory, found their only proper outlet in tears. Fathers—well—of course fathers never cried at weddings, because long before they were old enough to give boys and girls away they had usually mastered the art of consuming their own—well their own emotions; and if in these later days they do sometimes on such occasions use their pocket-handkerchiefs or clear their throats, it is because they have speeches to make, and wish to give fair play and sonorous expression to their thoughts and feelings. Pew openers and vergers are said to have cried in old days in proportion to the fees paid, or forgotten, and others again because they liked to, and nobody in the wide world could say why they should not do as they liked. Ladies and Gentlemen, under these depressing circumstances, I am happy in being able to propose to you a toast full of brightness and hope. You have already pledged the health of the bride of the present, it is mine to propose to you the toast of the brides of the future—the bridesmaids that adorn our festival to-day. Here we have roses that are ever sweet, lilies that are fair and full of grace, violets of fascinating modesty, and forget-me-nots that can never be forgotten. May they continue in the enjoyment of all their charms, and when they are picked to adorn some manly bosom, may they find bridegrooms who are worthy of them, and spheres of domestic felicity which they may long live to adorn. Ladies and Gentlemen, I give you "The Bridesmaids."

Christmas and New Year (*Gentlemen's Dinner*).

Gentlemen :

> "Solomon said—and he was a king—
> There's a time to dance and a time to sing,
> A time for joy, and a time for sorrow,
> And one's to-day and the other's to-morrow."

Whether Solomon put his thoughts in exactly this form, is perhaps open to doubt, but it is quite clear that he put things in their right order when he said :

> "A time for joy, and a time for sorrow,
> And one's to-day and the other's to-morrow."

Englishmen have a constitutional right to grumble, and Christmas places no limit upon their privileges, but to-night we are all disposed to take a favourable view of things, and we shall all be ready to admit that the year is full of jolly days for those who cherish the spirit of jollity.

New Year's Day begins the list, and red letters dot the calendar from first to last. Twelfth Night crowns a jolly day, and that before the new year is one week old. The first of April is a jolly day for saucy children and irresponsible youth, if sometimes not so jolly to children of larger growth. So much depends upon the point of view. The first of May is full of bright and appetising promises of jolly days to come—on road and river, on links, in courts and playing-fields, while the first of June works out the plan of May, and fills our hearts with music and our paths with flowers. July gives us many jolly days, if old St. Swithin but acts with some discretion. Then August bids us forth with bag and gun, and gives to all who take it a jolly 12th, when none but grouse need grouse.

September gives us picnics with the part-ridges, and October pleasant outings with the pheasant, while the huntsman with the cry of Tally Ho! bids us leap into the saddle and scour the countryside with Reynard ever ready for a run.

Then of another kind are the red-letter days we know as quarter days, though they give no quarter, and bring letters read with regret or satisfaction as they bring us bills that check our jollity or cheques that meet our bills.

Gentlemen, the chief of these is Christmas Day, the central day of the happy season, which now we celebrate around the Mahogany Tree:

> "Christmas is here:
>   Winds whistle shrill,
>   Icy and chill,
>   Little care we:
> Little we fear
>   Weather without,
>   Sheltered about
>   The Mahogany Tree.

> "Once on the boughs
>   Birds of rare plume
>   Sang, in its bloom;
>   Night-birds are we:
> Here we carouse,
>   Singing, like them,
>   Perched round the stem
>   Of the jolly old tree.

> "Here let us sport,
>   Boys, as we sit;
>   Laughter and wit
>   Flashing so free.

> Life is but short—
>   When we are gone,
>   Let them sing on
>   Round the old tree.
>
> "Evenings we knew,
>   Happy as this ;
>   Faces we miss,
>   Pleasant to see.
> Kind hearts and true,
>   Gentle and just,
>   Peace to your dust !
>   We sing round the tree.
>
> "Care, like a dun,
>   Lurks at the gate :
>   Let the dog wait ;
>   Happy we'll be !
> Drink, every one ;
>   Pile up the coals,
>   Fill the red bowls,
>   Round the old tree !
>
> "Drain we the cup.—
>   Friend, art afraid ?
>   Spirits are laid
>   In the Red Sea.
> Mantle it up,
>   Empty it yet ;
>   Let us forget,
>   Round the old tree.
>
> "Sorrows begone !
>   Life and its ills,
>   Duns and their bills
>   Bid me to flee.
> Come with the dawn,
>   Blue-devil sprite,
>   Leave us to-night
>   Round the old tree."—*W. M. Thackeray.*

Gentlemen, the toast is "Christmas," the central jolly day of two years full of them.

Christmas (*A Mixed Gathering*).

Ladies and Gentlemen, Christmas is with us once again. He comes to us with the same genial countenance and cheery greeting that we remember in our early childhood, that was the hope and joy of our callow youth, and that is associated with all that is best and brightest of what we know as the good old days :

Modern enterprise has changed the face of the earth, but the face of Christmas remains the same :

> "Heap on more wood !—the wind is chill ;
>   But let it whistle as it will,
> We'll keep our Christmas merry still."—*Scott.*

We all remember our children's birthdays, and they often remember ours, but the nativity that is never forgotten is the birthday of the

Christian world. And yet, older than that is the festival we celebrate to-day :

> " Each age has deemed the new-born year
>   The fittest time for festal cheer.''

The Romans in their saturnalia at the winter solstice kept nature's birthday—the birthday of all worldly hopes.

The savage Dane

> "High on the beach his galleys drew
>   And feasted all his pirate crew ;
>   Then in his low and pine-built hall,
>   Where shields and axes decked the wall,
>   They gorged upon the half-dressed steer,
>   Caroused in seas of table-beer . . .
>   As best might to the mind recall
>   The boisterous joys of Odin's hall.''

In later days, and under Christian auspices,

> " Domestic and religious rite
>   Gave honour to the holy night:
>   On Christmas eve the bells were rung ;
>   On Christmas eve the mass was sung ;
>   The damsel donned her kirtle sheen ;
>   The hall was dressed with holly green ;
>   Forth to the wood did merry-men go,
>   To gather in the mistletoe.

> "Then opened wide the baron's hall
>   To vassal, tenant, serf, and all;
>   Power laid his rod of rule aside
>   And Ceremony doffed his pride.
>   The heir, with roses in his shoes,
>   That night might village partner choose ;
>   The Lord, underogating, share
>   The vulgar game of ' post and pair.'
>   All hailed, with uncontrolled delight
>   And general voice, the happy night,
>   That to the cottage, as the crown,
>   Brought tidings of salvation down.

> "The fire, with well-dried logs supplied,
>   Went roaring up the chimney wide ;
>   The huge hall-table's oaken face,
>   Scrubbed till it shone the day to grace,
>   Bore then upon its massive board
>   No mark to part the squire and lord.
>   Then was brought in the lusty brawn,
>   By old blue-coated serving-man ;
>   Then the grim boar's head frowned on high,
>   Crested with bays and rosemary.''

In those days they had to catch the boar before they ate it. To-day we should fare ill were we dependent on our own catching. Times have changed and methods have altered with them, but human nature remains the same, and Christmas is human nature's festival. We live more strenuous lives these later times, and need the more the change and relaxations which Christmas sanctions. "All work and no play makes Jack a dull boy," and it is beyond philosophy to estimate the work-a-day value of an idle hour. As Scott says in the poem ("Marmion") I have already quoted :

> "England was merry England, when
> Old Christmas brought his sports again.
> 'Twas Christmas broached the mightiest ale,
> 'Twas Christmas told the merriest tale;
> A Christmas gambol oft could cheer
> The poor man's heart through half the year."

Ladies and Gentlemen, I give you the toast of "Christmas," its old associations, its present joys, and its inspiration for the years to come.

Christmas (*In the Home Circle*).

Ladies and Gentlemen, of all the days of all the year, there is no day that brings us nearer to each other than Christmas Day. We cannot approach a common centre without coming into nearer contact with each other, and if, as in the case of Christmas, the centre of attraction is a humanising and harmonising influence, the common nearness which it brings about can only foster happiness and peace.

Christmas is the great home-festival of the world. It brings the children back from school. It brings the sons and daughters from the near distance, and the wanderers from the ends of the earth. It unites all of one blood in the true spirit of kinship, the old and the young, the richer and the poorer. It is as though a truce were sounded amid the battle of life, and the time were, as it never is at any other, when if, as we are laying our gifts upon the altar we remember that our brother has aught against us, we seek first that reconciliation with the human which can alone make our gifts acceptable to the divine. It is the time when we come nearest to the observance of the golden rule and the following of the great commandment, "Thou shalt love thy neighbour as thyself." It is a time that softens asperities and revives friendships, that bridges the hiatus of estrangement, and calls to the renewal of love. It is the season of forgiveness and generosity, of kind gifts and good wishes; and if we but realise the Christmas spirit we shall be prepared to throw the

wide arms of our Christmas greeting round one
and all, and say with the poet :

> "Ye who have scorned each other,
>   Or injured friend or brother,
>   In this fast-fading year ;
> Ye who, by word or deed,
> Have made a kind heart bleed,
>   Come gather here.
>
> "Let sinned against, and sinning,
>   Forget their strife's beginning,
>   And join in friendship now,
> Be links no longer broken,
> Be sweet forgiveness spoken
>   Under the holly bough.
>
> "Ye who have loved each other,
>   Sister and friend and brother,
>   In this fast-fading year ;
> Mother and sire and child,
> Young man and maiden mild,
>   Come gather here ;
>
> "And let your hearts grow fonder
>   As memory shall ponder
>   Each past unbroken vow.
> Old love and younger wooing
> Are sweet in the renewing,
>   Under the holly bough.
>
> "Ye who have nourished sadness,
>   Estranged from hope and gladness,
>   In this fast-fading year ;
> Ye with o'erburdened mind,
> Made aliens from your kind,
>   Come gather here.
>
> "Let not the useless sorrow
>   Pursue you night and morrow ;
>   If e'er you hoped, hope now.
> Take heart, uncloud your faces,
> And join in our embraces
>   Under the holly bough."—*Charles Mackay.*

Ladies and Gentlemen, I give you the spirit
of Christmas.

New Year's Eve.

Ladies and Gentlemen, we stand upon the
threshold of a new year. Anno domini 19——
lies all behind us ; anno domini 19—— lies all
before. For the moment we wait the ringing
of the passing bell that we may "welcome the
coming, speed the parting guest."

"Time flies," the proverb tells us, but the
poet says :

> "Ah no !
> Alas, Time stays, we go ;
> Or else, were this not so,
>   What need to chain the hours,
>   For youth were always ours ?
> Time goes, you say ? ah no !"—*Austin Dobson*

And both are true, the proverb and the poem, but let it pass. We want no further problems for the old year to solve, and we will not enter the new one with a question that must lead to words. The foot of Time is ever on the march, whether he goes or not, and the foot-rule with which we have measured off the months of 19—— is nearing the exhaustion of its final inch.

Like its predecessors, it has been a year of lights and shadows for us all. It has had its ups and downs, its joys and sorrows, its failures and successes; and it will give us its greatest blessing as a parting gift if it leaves us with greater courage and increased strength to grapple with the vicissitudes of 19——.

Its retrospect is varied by individual experience; but few if any of us can look back upon it without seeing many bright and happy passages, even though they may be intertwined with shadowed paths.

In all years we have the better and the worse, the richer and the poorer, and they are the gatherers of the harvests of the years who learn the arts of that divine alchemy which turns all ill to good.

All years are cheered by the love of youth, inspired by the bravery of man and enheartened by the confidence of trusty friends. All these we have known in the year that now totters to its close.

> "Here's to the year that's awa':
>   We'll drink it in strong and in sma',
> And pledge with a glass ilka laddie and lass
>   We loved in the year that's awa'.
>
> "Here's to the soldier who bled
>   And the sailor who fought but to fa';
> Their fame is not dead tho' their spirits have fled
>   On the wings of the year that's awa'.
>
> "Here's to the kin that we love,
>   Afar o'er the sea and the plain,
> In ilk' colony yon, who were with us anon,
>   Who may never be with us again.
>
> "Here's to the friends that were true
>   In the days when the sun never shone;
> Whatever betide, may they ever abide
>   As they were in the year that is gone.
>
> "Here's to the good that survives
>   The toil and the trust of it all,
> And may all the ill of the year we fulfil
>   Depart with the year that's awa'."

3*

But, Ladies and Gentlemen, this is a double toast, and while we remember the good of the year that is gone, we must also pledge the health of the year about to follow.

There is always hope in new beginnings, and as we turn over new leaves with high resolves we may find many pleasant pages in the book of 19——.

> "Question not, but live and labour
>   Till yon goal be won,
>   Helping every feeble neighbour,
>   Seeking help from none.
> Life is mostly froth and bubble
>   Two things stand like stone—
> KINDNESS in another's trouble,
>   COURAGE in your own."

But the hour is at hand. The clock strikes twelve. The King is dead! Long live the King!

> "Ring out, wild bells, to the wild sky,
>   The flying cloud, the frosty light:
>   The year is dying in the night;
>   Ring out, wild bells, and let him die.
>
> "Ring out the old, ring in the new,
>   Ring, happy bells, across the snow:
>   The year is going, let him go;
>   Ring out the false, ring in the true.
>
> "Ring out the grief that saps the mind
>   For those that here we see no more;
>   Ring out the feud of rich and poor,
>   Ring in redress to all mankind.
>
> "Ring out a slowly dying cause,
>   And ancient forms of party strife;
>   Ring in the nobler modes of life,
>   With sweeter manners, purer laws.
>
> "Ring out the want, the care, the sin,
>   The faithless coldness of the times;
>   Ring out, ring out my mournful rhymes,
>   But ring the fuller minstrel in.
>
> "Ring out false pride in place and blood,
>   The civic slander and the spite;
>   Ring in the love of truth and right,
>   Ring in the common love of good.
>
> "Ring out old shapes of foul disease;
>   Ring out the narrowing lust of gold;
>   Ring out the thousand wars of old,
>   Ring in the thousand years of peace.
>
> "Ring in the valiant man and free,
>   The larger heart, the kindlier hand;
>   Ring out the darkness of the land,
>   Ring in the Christ that is to be."

A Chairman's Speech. (Philanthropic Meeting.)

Ladies and Gentlemen, it is a characteristic of our country, of which we have every right to be proud, that any meeting called for the purpose of alleviating suffering, of aiding thrift, of bettering the condition of the deserving poor, or in any way of helping " lame dogs over stiles " is sure of securing popular support, and I congratulate myself to-night on the fact that I have the honour to preside over so large and influential a gathering of wellwishers of a good cause. Some one has said—and I am glad to believe in the truth of the statement—that there is sufficient humanity in this country to deal with all its necessity if there were only a sufficient organisation to bring the one to bear upon the other without delay and without waste. If this be so, it becomes us to do our best to perfect our organisations, that they may inspire a generous public with sufficient confidence to provide the necessary means to accomplish this desirable end. What has already been accomplished in the past, in dealing with the class of need that we have met to consider to-night, the report of the secretary will doubtless show, and what remains to be accomplished in the same direction is not likely to escape his practical observation. For my own part I hope that we shall all prove that we have a real interest in the purpose of this meeting, and that as a result of our gathering together here this evening the suffering may be soothed, the sorrowing may be cheered, the needy may be helped, the struggling may be encouraged, and that all who show mercy will prove for themselves that " the quality of mercy is not strained, but is twice blessed "—blessing him that gives and him that takes.

A platform wit once said that a chairman's duty on such occasions as this was fourfold. He said " It is the Chairman's duty to Stand Up, to Speak Up, to Stump Up, and then to Shut Up." On another occasion he limited the duties to three, and these were, " to Look Sunny, to Talk Honey, and to Give Money." Ladies and Gentlemen, I have been standing up for some time, I have been speaking up to the best of my ability, I am quite ready to stump up according to my means, and am now looking forward to relieving both you and myself by shutting up at the earliest possible moment.

A Chairman's Speech. (Business Meeting.)

Ladies and Gentlemen, there are two duties that belong to every chairman, and therefore two which devolve upon me to-night. The first is that of maintaining order, and the second that of announcing from time to time the progress of the business. Neither of these duties involves me in any difficulty on this occasion. The spirit of order is too clearly reflected in the faces of the highly intelligent and good-tempered company I see before me, to permit of any fear of disturbance. And the agenda is perfectly safe under the supervision of the courteous and efficient secretary who occupies a seat at my elbow. Under these circumstances, I can, with confidence, anticipate a careful consideration of the various matters which it will be my duty to bring before you, and a hearty, and I hope a unanimous adoption of the proposals which will be submitted for your approval.

The Firm (*A Social Gathering*).

My first words this evening shall be words of welcome, and I hope you will need no assurance of the pleasure I feel in meeting those who are associated with me in business around the social board.

We are all of us partners in a commercial enterprise, the success of which is our common aim. We occupy different positions, and our duties vary in character and importance, and yet all are necessary to the efficiency and success of the whole.

I often think that a business enterprise is very much like a voyage at sea. The good ship may be berthed in Mincing Lane or Cannon Street, by the river-side or on the banks of a canal, and good docks or premises are as necessary as a good ship in attempting the voyage of success. In the equipment of a ship there are officers and crew, and as these are efficient in the management of dock and vessel the voyage will be prosperous or not. The first of these officers is necessarily the Captain, and I need hardly say that as captain of this firm I am proud of the ship that carries me, and the crew that sails under my orders. Next to the Captain comes the first officer, who takes care of the vessel when the captain is absent from duty; he is the captain's confidant, and has to further the captain's orders. With a good mate to carry out his instructions and further his wishes, the captain's work is made easier and more pleasant than it might be.

Of the other officers, few or many, I must not stay to speak in detail, and yet the purser must not be forgotten. The purser, you know, is the officer who distributes the financial rewards which we all find so grateful and comforting. It is to him we look for that monetary encouragement which we all feel so necessary to our happiness. For my part I always try to keep on good terms with the purser; and when the enterprises of the year are reckoned up and the log-books are over-hauled, I look with inquiring anxiety into the genial face of the purser to try and catch a glimpse of that benign expression which promises an increase of my salary. If I see it broaden out into a smile of satisfaction I know that my wages will be raised, but if he shakes his head I see that I have to work another year before I can expect an increase. Seeing how much our fortunes are in the purser's hands, I am sure we shall all wish him a happy and successful career.

But the captain and the officers would not be able to make much progress if the ship were not manned with an able and willing crew. Gentlemen, I put it to you that here is the secret of success—a good ship bound on healthy enterprises, with good officers and a loyal crew, all working together with one object—a happy and successful voyage. Gentlemen, your prosperity and mine are indissolubly bound together, and the co-operation of the humblest worker is necessary to the general good. The purser may watch the cash box with the utmost vigilance, but we must all remember that it is the "mickles that make the muckle," and small economies that make for increased profits. Every penny wasted is a penny out of the profits, and every penny out of profits reduces the margin out of which increases of salary can be made. Knowing and feeling this, I ask you all to join with me in drinking to and working for the health and prosperity of the firm.

Votes of Thanks—The Chairman (Smoking Concert).

(Ladies and) Gentlemen, some one has said " There are no pleasures we enjoy that do not involve us in obligations, and side by side with all our enjoyments there are duties which we are called upon to perform." If this be so, I am sure we shall all recognise the fact that the pleasure and enjoyment we have had to-night, under the able chairmanship of our worthy president, demands of us all the hearty and unanimous vote of thanks which it is now my privilege to propose.

It is not necessary for me, nor would it be becoming on my part, to attempt the enumeration of the many qualities which excite our admiration and command our respect. That he should have accepted so readily and discharged so ably the duties of his important office are sufficient grounds upon which to unite in performing a duty which is in itself a pleasure, and if you want another reason why we should join with enthusiasm in thanking him for his genial service, I will give it to you in the words of the poet,

> " For he's a jolly good fellow,
> And so say all of us."

To the Secretary (Sports Club).

Ladies and Gentlemen, those of us who join clubs and societies of this kind with the main purpose of promoting our own pleasure and amusement, should be the first to recognise how largely we are indebted to those who contribute so much to our comfort and convenience by undertaking the clerical work and managerial responsibility. When we enter the cricket field, the tennis ground, the croquet lawn or the bowling green, and find the wickets pitched, the courts marked, the grass mown and all things ready for our enjoyment, we do not always remember how much we owe to those who are content to do the drudgery by which we profit, and who, however perverse the clerk of the weather may be, are always at their posts to make the best that may be, out of the worst that is.

But for " hewers of wood " we should have no bats and wickets to play with, and but for

" drawers of water," no faultless pitches and
sport-inviting grounds ; but beyond these, whose
services are seldom overpaid, there are those
whose work is never fully requited, who volun-
tarily and without reward fulfil the offices of
government—Prime Minister, Chancellor of the
Exchequer, Home and Foreign Secretary, or who
sit upon committees—for diplomatic service.

With all this work done freely for our comfort and
convenience, we should indeed be
wanting in the slightest claim upon its con-
tinuance, were we not ready on an occasion like
this to testify our appreciation and express our
gratitude.

Ladies and Gentlemen, in the name of the
sport we love, and the enjoyment we derive
from its pursuit, I ask you to join me in this vote
of thanks to the secretary and the other honorary
officers of this club.

To the Returning Officer (an Election).

(Ladies and) Gentlemen, As the (senior) successful candidate in the election which has just
taken place, I desire to exercise the right and
privilege conceded by all parties on such occasions to those who occupy that position, of moving
a hearty vote of thanks to the returning officer
for the manner in which he has discharged
the duties of his office.

At election times, when competition is keen,
and asperities are not uncommon, it is satisfactory
to all parties to know that there is one person
who remains unaffected by the turmoil of controversy and unperturbed by the personalities
which sometimes embitter strife—one person
who maintains the attitude of the sphinx, the
discipline of a field marshal, the organisation
of an army service corps, the dignity of a judge,
the integrity of an archbishop, and the courtesy
of a master of the ceremonies, and that is the
returning officer, whose wise arrangements and
business methods have smoothed the way for
the better and the worse in the contest which he
has just brought to a close.

For my own part I must express myself as
being as well contented with the procedure as I
am satisfied with the result, and I am happy in
feeling sure that while my opponent may not be
as well pleased with the issue as I confess I

am, he will none the less join heartily with me in thanking the returning officer for the completeness of his arrangements, the efficiency of his staff, and the promptness of his return. Ladies and Gentlemen, I beg to move a hearty vote of thanks to the returning officer.

To the Returning Officer (seconding the Vote).

Ladies and Gentlemen, though I have been sharply opposed to my honourable friend the mover of this vote of thanks for some time past, I am happy to-night in finding myself in entire agreement with him on at least one subject, and that is the appreciation of public service, wisely, honestly, and efficiently rendered. There are compensations in all our disappointments, and whatever regrets I may have with regard to the result of this election, I shall always look back with pleasure and satisfaction upon the manner of its conduct, and it is quite within the range of possibility that I may some day prove my appreciation of the services of the Returning Officer by asking for their employment again. I have much pleasure in seconding the proposal.

DEATH AT THE FEAST.

FROM Memphis old
  A message clear,
The end behold
  Of all things here !

Of song and measure,
  Wail and woe ;
Of wealth and pleasure,
  Pain and throe ;

Of pride and wealth,
  A final fall ;
Who comes by stealth
  Low levels all !

And ringing after
  Echo's cheers,
Ribald laughter,
  Gibes and jeers.

Memento mori !
  The mentor saith :
The feast of Life
  The fast of Death.—A. H. M.

PUBLIC SPEAKING

In these days when opportunities of public speaking are more numerous than formerly, and when civic and political obligations often demand public comment, it is well worth while for any who have views, and who desire to influence others, to cultivate a readiness of utterance, and a fluency of speech which will at least save the cause they favour from suffering by default, and which may enable them to express their opinions with convincing educational effect. It is much to be regretted that elocution and the art of public speaking have no adequate place in our educational systems, and that proficiency in oral address should be left to the chance practice afforded by debating societies, unsupported by scientific instruction and private study, and this while a man's education can scarcely be said to be complete until he is able to say everything he may need to say without the thing said suffering from the manner of its saying.

The First Necessity of Speaking is something to say. The writer can remember his boyhood's ambition to become an effective speaker. He can recall his early efforts to write, learn, and deliver speeches on, to him, great occasions, and he has not forgotten their varying success ; but he also remembers that the real turning-point in his career as a speaker was reached when he became convinced that the reason why he could not speak with the readiness and fluency he so much admired in others, was because he had nothing to say. The old formula derived from Bacon, **Reading makes a full man,** writing makes an exact man, and speaking—or, as Bacon puts it, conference—makes a ready man holds good, and the proverb, " Out of the fullness of the heart the mouth speaketh," is still true. To be full of a subject is the first necessity of being able to speak at any length upon it, but it is not the only necessity. A man may possess the best box of tools in the county, and may be perfectly informed in the theory of their use, but lacking practical experience may be quite incapable of their mechanical employment. Some of our most learned men have been among our most **ineffective speakers.** The late Lord Kelvin knew perhaps more about his own department of science than any other man of his time, but there were many of his contemporaries who knew less who could impart more. He lacked the literary and rhetorical gifts which made the lectures and writings of Professor Huxley, and others, so interesting and instructive. There is a story told of Lord Kelvin which the writer repeats from memory. His classes at the University are said to have suffered from his inability easily to communicate the knowledge with which his mind was so amply stored, and on the occasion of his visit to London to receive a mark of royal favour in the form of a title, this deficiency on his part was evidenced in a very amusing way. During his absence his place was occupied by Professor Day, and a witty student is said to have posted a notice in the quadrangle exhorting his fellow students to make the most of their opportunity in the words, "Work while it is Day, for the (k)night cometh when no man can work." Fullness of knowledge, if the first necessity of public speaking, is not the last; readiness is necessary to effective speaking, and exactness to permanent influence.

That the reverse often obtains is of course true. There are full men who are not ready men, and there are ready men who are full of nothing, unless it be their own conceit. "Empty vessels make the most sound," the proverb says, and the windy, wordy piffle which some parliamentary orators pour forth by the hour serves no other purpose than that of emptying the House and delaying public business. As the latter is the object these speakers usually have in view, there is a sense in which this class of oratory may be said to be effective, but in this article the term is used in a more serious sense. The object of worthy speech is not to defeat an opponent, but to convince him, and in this trickery can have no part. Knowledge, accuracy, clearness, and sincerity are the convincing factors.

Readiness of Speech is largely a matter of practice, and local parliaments and debating societies afford excellent opportunities for it. Given more or less fullness of knowledge, the art of readiness is that of selecting quickly just so much of the fullness as may be necessary to accomplish the current purpose, without sacrificing weight or overburdening effort. The inexperienced sculler in his anxiety to make pace often shows "more haste than good speed" by digging his oars so deeply that he cannot move, or so lightly that he performs the evolution known as "catching a crab." The art of rowing is, while confident of the power of the deeps to sustain the craft, to skim the surface, using just so much of it as will serve progress, and not sufficient to retard movement. The speaker also whilst supported by fullness of knowledge, must learn the art of manipulating his oars, that wit may flash from the dancing spray while music murmurs from the rolling deep. The best precept that we can give to both oarsman and orator is the old proverb, "Practice makes perfect."

Exactness in Speech is the element that gives to it its permanent value, and all great speakers are at considerable pains to observe accuracy. **Writing makes the exact man,** says the old formula, and most successful orators commit to paper the leading points of their arguments and the crowning sentences of their perorations. Some men go so far as to write out their speeches from beginning to end, for the purpose of fixing the line of thought in their minds. Others supplement this by committing the whole to memory, that they may have the actor's freedom in declamation. Others again find a half-sheet of note-paper with the main divisions of the speech indicated by single sentences, sufficient to keep them on the line of argument. **The art of delivery** is very largely the art of making notes—neither too few nor too many, but, few or many, so distinct that they can be seen at a glance, and so clear that they will not confuse on reference.

Speakers who have given some attention to elocution may be trusted to read their speeches, and some do this so effectively, that their audiences have no idea that they are reading. This is of course more commonly done in the pulpit than on the platform. In either case it is best that the MS. should be written on one side of the paper only, and that when finished the page should be removed sideways to one side, as this can be done without observation from the audience, while turning over pages continually calls the attention of the audience to the fact that a manuscript is being read. The disadvantage of reading a speech from MS. is that the speaker is not so ready to deal with interruptions, or to take advantage of the unforeseen, or incorporate matter suggested by other speakers without displaying awkwardness in interpolation, unless he is also a skilful impromptu speaker. Fullness and readiness are both required in this combination. The full man who is also ready is easily king of the platform, and can afford, not to do without a manuscript, but to leave it at home.

Writing helps to the condensation and arrangement of matter, and hence to the order of speech. The time taken in **the preparation of a speech** varies, of course, with the circumstances, the occasion, and the gifts of the speaker. A well-read man who is also a ready speaker may be willing and able to speak upon a subject with which he is familiar at a very short notice, if he is not limited to time, but if a short speech is required on a large subject, a longer time is necessary for preparation. An old Scotch minister was once asked how long he would require to prepare a speech. His answer was, "That depends upon the time the speech is to occupy. If I am to speak for a quarter of an hour, I should like a week's notice; if for half an hour, I could do with three days; if I can go on as long as I like, I am ready now." This story carries its own moral.

One advantage of a written MS. is that after delivery it becomes a permanent record, and the writer of it will often secure a better report in the press than would probably appear if it depended upon the shorthand notes of the reporter. Professor Blackie used to tell an amusing story of the only speech he ever produced in manuscript. He was asked to speak at a banquet on a certain special occasion, and promised to say a few words. He was told that that would not do, he must prepare a great speech, and build it up architecturally. He did so, and on entering the room handed the MS. to the reporters. It happened that other speakers preceded him, and that by the time his turn arrived the hour had grown late. On being called upon he concluded that his great speech would be quite out of place at so late an hour, and so said his few words, and as he left the room, cautioned the reporters against using his MS. The caution, however, came too late. By that time the great speech was already in type, and the next morning the only speech of the evening which was reported in full was the one that was never delivered.

Nervousness is a characteristic of temperament which makes for its own perpetuation. In itself it is not to be deprecated, but it is important that it should be brought under the discipline of the will. All sensitive natures are nervous, and natures which are not sensitive lack some of the finer qualities of the mind. Genius is always sensitive. Nervousness when allowed to develop uncontrolled and cherished as a virtue, as it sometimes is, leads to mental and physical wreckage and becomes a permanent torture to the sufferer and an unmitigated nuisance to others. It defeats its own end if it anticipates occasion and broods unduly upon its own cause. To anticipate to-day the nervousness likely to embarrass the discharge of a duty to-morrow, and to hold it in the mind like a long note with a crescendo mark above it, will not only insure the final embarrassment but make it more prominently apparent. Many unpleasant things have their uses. Pain is unpleasant, but it has its mission. Pain is a message to the brain from the part affected, calling for immediate attention, and the sooner the message of pain is answered, the sooner the body is at ease. Worry is unpleasant, but, like pain, it immediately calls for its own removal. In a large number of cases it is simply a sense of duty neglected or work undone; and these demand discharge and execution. Nervousness in like manner, if accepted for what it is, and acted upon for what it is worth, will naturally

work out its own salvation. **Nervousness is**
commonly **a sense of unreadiness** for occasion or
unfitness for duty, and as such it is a timely call
for preparation. To be forewarned is to be
forearmed; and if the forewarning nervousness
is taken as a hint, and leads to the determined
control of the will employed in preparing for the
event, the occasion may be left to take care of
itself, but if allowed to develop uncontrolled,
it is likely to crown the opportunity with
disaster. Confidence is the proper qualification
of nervousness, and confidence comes of fitness,
which is the result of preparation.

The first thing to be done in dealing with a
difficulty is to look it squarely in the face.
Commonly, to the nervous, "things are not what
they seem," and when we are frightened by
appearances, our first business is to realise
actualities. Charles Mackay says of these
apparitions, which are commonly one part real
and three parts imagination:

> " Such giants come to strike us dumb,
>   But, weak in every part,
>   They melt before the strong man's eyes
>   And fly the true of heart."

Of the larger preparation for the more important duties of public life we have already
treated at length, and the **fullness, exactness,
and readiness acquired by reading, writing, and
discussion** will serve the student on all occasions,
large and small; but without this elaborate
preparation there ought to be little difficulty in
discharging the simple duties which fall to the
lot of many. Commonly we exaggerate what
is required of us, and underestimate our own
ability to respond to the demand; hence, when
the occasion arises we look far afield for the
materials which, as a matter of fact, lie nearest
to our hand.

On receiving a testimonial men are often
embarrassed beyond all expression, and blunder
through a few incoherencies to an ignominious
collapse. And yet very little is required of them.
Their one duty is to say " Thank you," and yet
this is sometimes entirely forgotten. The two
words by themselves would doubtless form a
somewhat bald acknowledgment, but they may
be easily rounded off in a sentence or two, such

as : "Ladies and gentlemen, from the bottom of my heart I thank you for your handsome gift, and for the kind expressions of regard with which you have accompanied it. Were I conscious of deserving them more, I should probably have more confidence in making this acknowledgment, but no words could express my appreciation; and so, with your generous forbearance, I will simply say again, Ladies and gentlemen, from the bottom of my heart I thank you." Of course the real subject-matter of the speech should rise out of the circumstances of the occasion and the remarks delivered by the speaker in making the presentation, but where the speaker cannot trust himself to speak at length, some such brief acknowledgment as the foregoing will serve the purpose sufficiently.

On receiving a vote of thanks for services rendered during a term of office, a secretary of a society will sometimes feel nonplussed when all he has to say when returning thanks (always the first duty) is that, but for the cordial co-operation of the members the work would have been much more onerous in execution, and much less satisfactory in results. This may often be suitably rounded off by the expression of a hope that these cordial relationships may be continued in the future, and that, as a result of united efforts, greater prosperity may follow.

Speech is one of the first faculties affected by nervousness, and hence more than any other exercise calls for preparation beforehand and care in delivery. The careful manipulation of the letter H is necessary when the emphatic and the unemphatic pronunciation come in awkward juxtaposition. A word too should be said for the preservation of the final letter in words that end with "ing."

The dangers of Alliteration also need to be pointed out. A number of amusing illustrations of this may easily be given. A clergyman once in attempting to say " Bow not thy knee to an idol," said " Bow not thine eye to a needle "; another is said to have asked his congregation to " behold the wig tree, how it fithereth away "; and a third is credited with using the phrase " cattlehoppers and grassipillars innumerable "; and a fourth with declaring that " it is easier for a rich man to pass through the eye of a needle, than for a camel to enter the kingdom of heaven." Another instance is that of the preacher who, referring to the conscience, and urging his hearers to recognise the inward voice in the half-formed wishes of the mind, appealed to them whether they had not all of them at one time or another felt within themselves the effect of a half-warmed fish.

It was nervousness of this kind which led the young bridegroom to ask a verger whether it was "kistomary to cuss the bride" after the marriage ceremony, and later, when told that he must reply to the toast of the bride and bridegroom at the reception, to stand up, and, placing his hand upon his bride's shoulder, say, "You know, ladies and gentlemen, this thing has been thrust upon me," and this when all he need have said was "Ladies and gentlemen, on behalf of my wife and myself, I beg to thank you for all your kind wishes, and to express the hope that they may be realised in the experience of all those who may follow our example."

That these are occasions upon which we should all desire to acquit ourselves well, but for which in the nature of things we can have little other than general preparation, is of course true. One can imagine, for instance, that there can be no occasion upon which a girl would more desire to be and look her best than at the ceremony and celebration of her marriage, and yet in the nature of things it is an ordeal for which she can have little or no previous experience to guide her. What is true in this instance is true in others; and we can only hope that in all such cases reasonable general preparation may induce sufficient self-confidence to enable alert sensitiveness to adapt itself to even the most trying circumstances.

Dutch Courage. The use of alcoholic stimulants to counteract nervousness is, at least, unwise. It is commonly to proceed from bad to worse. Anthony Trollope in his "Dr. Thorne," in dealing with the coming of age of Frank Gresham, one of his characters, makes the hero's cousin George, who is supposed to be an accomplished after-dinner speaker, recommend him to fix his eye upon one of the bottles and never move it—the eye, that is, not the bottle. So far the advice is good, for the wandering eye courts distraction. But Frank Gresham's own idea of fixing the gaze upon the head of one of the company is better, and some able speakers have made it a practice to pick out some intelligent-looking person in the centre of the audience and address themselves entirely to him. With regard to the bottle, undoubtedly the advice of Solomon is the best : " Look not upon the wine when it is red," and until after the delivery of the speech at any rate it is just as well to observe the same rule with regard to the white. The action of alcohol is to close the cells of the brain, and to begin by closing those which affect the higher faculties. It thus attacks the will, the judgment, and the cautionary powers first, and in doing this deprives the lower powers of the control they need to keep them in wise restraint. In this way alcohol, which begins by loosening the tongue ,often proceeds to loosen the fists and commonly ends by loosening the legs. Some wit has said :

> " Here is a riddle most abstruse ;
>   Canst read the answer right ?
> Why is it that my tongue grows loose
>   Only when I grow tight ?"

The tongue loosened under the influence of alcohol pays for its freedom with disabilities which far out-balance the apparent advantage. Some great writers have produced " copy " on a bottle of brandy a day, and some distinguished speakers have made frequent use of the decanter in the process of their orations; but the best work is never produced in this way, and those who desire to achieve the best that is possible to them under any circumstances will be well advised to keep all their faculties unimpaired for the effort.

The Bishop's Answer (Wilberforce).

" I've asked so many touts and guides,
    Who've various answers given,
Tell me, oh jolly sobersides,
    The way to heaven ? "

His eyes with merry thoughts were bright,
    " His face with wisdom shone,
Take the first turning to the right,
    And keep straight on."—A. H. M.

ROTTEN ROW—*H. S. Leigh.*

THERE'S a tempting bit of greenery—of *rus in
    urbe* scenery—
  That's haunted by the London " upper ten " ;
Where, by exercise on horseback, an equestrian
    may force back
  Little fits of *tedium vitæ* now and then.

Oh ! the times that I have been there, and the
    types that I have seen there
  Of that gorgeous Cockney animal, the swell ;
And the scores of pretty riders (both patricians
    and outsiders)
  Are considerably more than I can tell.

When first the warmer weather brought these
    people all together,
  And the crowds began to thicken through the
    Row,
I reclined against the railing on a sunny day,
    inhaling
  All the spirits that the breezes could bestow.

And the riders and the walkers and the thinkers
    and the talkers
  Left me lonely in the thickest of the throng,
Not a touch upon my shoulder—not a nod from
    one beholder—
  As the stream of Art and Nature went along.

But I brought away one image, from that
    fashionable scrimmage,
  Of a figure and a face—ah, *such* a face !
Love has photographed the features of that
    loveliest of creatures
  On my memory, as Love alone can trace.

Did I hate the little dandy in his whiskers (they
    were sandy),
  Whose absurd salute was honoured by a smile ?
Did I marvel at his rudeness in presuming on
    her goodness,
  When she evidently loathed him all the while ?

Oh ! the hours that I have wasted, the regrets
    that I have tasted,
  Since the day (it seems a century ago)
When my heart was non-instanter by a lady in
    a canter
  On a certain sunny day in Rotten Row.

OTHER SOCIAL FUNCTIONS

The Breakfast is the first meal of the day, and is the least formal, although formal invitations are often given. The breakfast hour varies; from 9 a.m. till noon being regarded as available. Ten or 11 o'clock a.m. is perhaps the most convenient hour, and hence the most popular one. The guests assemble in the drawing-room and proceed informally to the breakfast-room at a signal from the hostess, who, in company with the lady of highest rank, leads the way. Ladies first, and gentlemen after, is the order observed, the host following with the gentlemen. There is no taking arms in proceeding, and little or no allotment of seats at the table. Precedence of rank is always observed, but not on these occasions with the rigid formality observed at dinner parties. At breakfasts, as at luncheons, the gentlemen are expected to distribute themselves as far as possible among the company, that the ladies may be fairly equally divided. This is necessary, because the hour of holding these gatherings renders it impossible for the hostess to guarantee the presence of an equal number of gentlemen and ladies. When the company is limited to gentlemen, the host leads the way to table with the guests of higher rank, and points out to them the seats he desires them to occupy. The other gentlemen then appropriate the remaining seats. The provisions are much the same as at luncheons, and the service similar. Tea, coffee, fish, entrées, game, and various cold dishes are handed round. Breakfast is a short meal, and the guests leave soon after its conclusion.

The Luncheon is a social feast, which has greatly increased in favour and acceptance of recent years. It is less formal than the dinner, and gives the host and hostess an opportunity of entertaining guests on a larger, and yet less exacting scale. Many people regard luncheon as an "open" meal, giving formal as well as verbal and general invitations, and commonly welcoming any intimate friend or acquaintance who casually drops in. The formal invitation seldom exceeds a week's notice. Invited guests announce themselves as such; on arriving at the house, uninvited guests inquire whether the hostess is at home. They then follow the attendant to the drawing-room, where they are announced as on all similar occasions. Gentlemen leave their outdoor garments and appurtenances in the hall, and ladies remove their coats and furs, but not their hats, which they continue to wear at the luncheon table. Elbow gloves are also retained at table, but short gloves are removed. Introductions before or during luncheon are informal and general, one guest being introduced to half a dozen others by one act. The adult luncheon is commonly the children's dinner, and the governess and the children of the house frequently take their place at table. Half-past one is the usual hour.

As in the case of breakfasts, there is no pairing off beforehand, and proceeding arm-in-arm to the luncheon table. On hearing the gong, or receiving an intimation that the luncheon is served, the hostess invites the most distinguished lady guest to lead the way, and proceeds to accompany her. The other ladies follow and the gentlemen bring up the rear. The hostess takes her place at the head of the table, and the host at the bottom, as at breakfast and dinner.

> " What is a table richly spread,
>   Without a woman at its head ? "—WHARTON.

Late comers, as at dinners, are conducted straight to the table, where they first make peace with the hostess, and then take any vacant seat that may be open to them.

The less formal conditions of the luncheon make it a more sociable meal than the dinner. Conversation is much more general, and host and hostess are less limited in their intercourse with the guests as a whole.

Luncheon over, the hostess gives the signal for the ladies to retire in the same manner as at the end of a dinner, and the gentleman nearest the door opens it for their exit. When the host is not present, the gentlemen also proceed to the drawing-room, where coffee is sometimes served. When the host is present, the gentle-men commonly remain with him for a short time, but luncheon parties usually break up shortly after the conclusion of the meal.

The Promenade.—In riding or driving the rule is to keep to the left-hand side of the road, in walking the pedestrian keeps to the right. If accompanied by a lady, he must give her the inside place, whether that be on his right or left hand. Though commonly ladies walk alone with perfect safety, and many glory in their independence, when accompanied by a gentleman a lady is supposed to be more or less under his protection, and etiquette demands that he should recognise this. It is his place to see that she is not unduly inconvenienced by other pedestrians, to walk near her side, and only to vacate that position for a moment by stepping behind her when it is necessary to allow other ladies to pass. If it be necessary for any one to vacate the path to let ladies pass, it is of course the gentleman who must do so. RECOGNITION IN PASSING.—On meeting persons one knows—more or less—care should be taken not to presume on a too slight acquaintance, and not to fail in the return of even a slight salute. On the principles of chivalry, it is for the lady to determine the measure of intimacy that she is willing to permit, and for the gentleman to loyally observe the limits she may impose. The measure of recognition permissible in public will of course depend upon the measure of intimacy observed in private. If the lady makes no sign of recognition, the gentleman should make none, and the degree of familiarity shown by the lady may be taken as the measure of that which may be shown in response. In recognising a lady's salute, the hat should be raised, and a slight bow made. In recognising a gentleman, a nod is commonly sufficient between equals of age or standing, but when youth meets maturity, the lifting of the hat and the inclination of the head are not out of place. On meeting a gentleman one knows who is accompanied by a lady one does not know, the hat must be raised, and the bow made. When walking with a lady, a gentleman should always raise his hat, and bow when passing every one, lady or gentleman, whom his companion may salute. This is not so much a personal compliment to the third party as an act of acquiescence in the compliment of one's companion, and as such is better performed without any attempt to catch the eye of the unknown. Such meetings are not good occasions for introductions, so, and unless special reasons obtain, the salute should be made in passing. It is always bad taste to leave a lady to stand or proceed alone while the two gentlemen pause to converse. All salutes should be returned, even if the person saluted does not recall the identity of the one saluting. A bold stare or a direct cut can only be justified by extraordinary circumstances, and if the cut is not intended, it is necessary to avoid the appearance of evil. In the ordinary way, it is better to chance an unnecessary politeness to a stranger than to risk an inadvertent slight to a friend.

When misunderstandings arise in such connection, allowance should be made for short-sighted persons, and others who are apt to lose themselves in what is called "a brown study." Estrangements have often followed upon half-recognitions and failures to return acknowledgments which are wholly attributable to such causes. Whether acquaintances on meeting should stop and converse is a matter which must be determined by the lady. On repassing a person once recognised, it is not necessary to repeat the formula. On recognising a friend approaching from a distance, it is not necessary to commence a smile which shall broaden at a polite crescendo until meeting half way. It is better to delay the recognition until within reasonable saluting distance.

When apologising to a lady for any accidental inconvenience or annoyance the hat should be raised, and the words "I beg your pardon" used. "Sorry" is a slovenly equivalent, which should only be permitted among men. The hat should also be raised after any trifling service rendered to strangers, such as helping a lady across a road or pointing out the way.

A gentleman should always remember that "his sisters, his cousins, and his aunts," not to mention his mother and his wife, are none the less ladies because they are relatives, and that as such they are entitled to at least equal consideration with that shown to others of their sex.

Morning Dress, concerning which directions are given on page 186, is the proper costume for the promenade, and for morning occupations other than those of sport, each form of which, like riding, motoring, and cycling, determines its own costume with a view to its special circumstances. Gloves should be worn, as on all outdoor occasions in town, and sticks may be carried so they be not held wrong end up, or under the arm, and are not swung round and round to the danger of the public. Unless necessary for support, sticks are out of place when attending church.

Smoking is permissible when walking alone, provided the habit can be indulged in without inconvenience or annoyance to others. Expectoration is, of course, out of the question, and care must be taken not to allow the smoke to blow into the faces of passers-by. When walking with a lady her permission must be asked before lighting up, and should not be asked if smoking is known to be objectionable to her. Smoking is better relinquished altogether on crowded promenades, and when numbers are fewer it is no impoliteness to remove a cigar or a cigarette from the mouth when passing near to a lady. In closed carriages smoking should not be practised, and in motor-cars and open carriages it should be limited to the back seat, unless all the occupants are smoking. Indoors, when ladies are present, permission must always be asked, and at dinners should never be indulged in until the word is given by the host or chairman, and this is never done in public until after the toast of the King has been honoured.

> " Sublime tobacco, which from East to West
>   Cheers the tar's labour, or the Turkman's rest;
>   Which on the Moslem's ottoman divides
>   His hours, and rivals opium and his brides;
>   Magnificent in Stamboul, but less grand,
>   Though not less loved, in Wapping or the Strand;
>   Divine in hookahs, glorious in a pipe,
>   When tipped with amber, mellow, rich, and ripe:
>   Like other charmers, wooing the caress
>   More dazzlingly when daring in full dress;
>   Yet thy true lovers more admire by far
>   Thy naked beauties—Give me a cigar!"
>   LORD BYRON, *The Island.*

The Morning Call is paid in the afternoon, the dinner-hour being, as we have already seen, the meridian of the fashionable day. The interval between lunch and dinner affords the opportunity, and the best hour is from four to five o'clock. Any time from 3.30 to 5.30 or even 6 p.m. is available, but late calls are liable to interfere with dressing for dinner or preparing for other evening engagements. The call is complimentary. It is the way that those who would have friends show themselves friendly. Many hostesses have regular " At-Home " days, and these should be observed where possible, but this does not preclude the privilege of calling on other days, if more convenient and the caller is prepared for disappointment. In the event of the lady being absent from home, the visitor leaves cards for both host and hostess and departs, sometimes, it is to be feared, with a sense of relief—sometimes a sadder and a wiser man. If the lady is at home, the caller proceeds under convoy of the attendant to the drawing-room, leaving his umbrella and outer garments, if weather-stained, in the hall, but otherwise carrying his hat and stick with him—it is merely a call, and he is not expecting or expected to stay more than twenty minutes or so. On reaching the drawing-room he will be duly announced, or let us hope he will. *Sotto-voce* communications are not always distinct, and many persons have to console themselves for disfigured nomenclature, with the reflection that " the rose by any other name, would smell as sweet." (Foote, accompanied by two ladies, was once announced at a reception as " Mr. Foote and the Misses Feet.") On his announcement, the hostess will turn to welcome him. If she offers him her hand, he will of course accept it, his own having been previously ungloved for the purpose. If she merely bows he will do the same, as his greeting must correspond with hers. After a few moments' conversation with him, the attention of his hostess will be required, probably by new arrivals or other guests to whom she may desire to speak. This leaves him free to make himself generally agreeable, recognising acquaintances according to the measure of intimacy with a bow or by shaking hands. When introduced to a stranger, it is always

safe to bow, and leave the offer of the hand to
the other party. Under all circumstances the
offered hand must be accepted. The common
obligation to help the host and hostess in the
entertainment of their guests as far as possible
may involve him in handing round refreshments,
and certainly in seeing that the ladies in his
immediate neighbourhood are not neglected
by those who may be appointed to this duty.
It is his politely to contribute to the comfort
of the ladies present without diffidence and
without fuss. When time to leave, he should
shake hands with or merely bow to the hostess
as she may determine, and bow to any others
who may be near enough to salute without fuss,
and then make his exit as quietly as possible,
leaving cards in the hall as he passes out. Ladies
always take precedence of gentlemen at social
functions, and when accompanying a gentleman,
must be allowed to precede him on entry, and to
determine the time to leave. Of course the
visitor who calls without notice takes his
chance of finding the hostess absent from home,
and he has no right to feel offended if, while
present in the house, she instructs her servants
to answer her "not at home for the purpose of
a call." The lady must always be considered
first, and no gentleman would wish to obtrude
his presence on a lady to her inconvenience.
At the same time, her presence in absence need
not be too much in evidence, as most people
are sensitive on such points, and a suspected
slight is not a pleasant matter for reflection.
Resentment caused under such circumstances
is well illustrated in the humorous stanza
which follows :

> " As he stood at her door one windy day,
>   As the tempest roared without,
> Above the clatter he heard her say,
>   ' John ! tell him that I am out.'
> As the door was opened with stately ease,
>   He said to the butler tall,
> ' My compliments to your lady, please,
>   And tell her I did not call.' "

Card Leaving is one of the most important
and yet one of the least popular of social duties.
Its formality makes it irksome, at least to men,
and yet, being a formality, it need not involve
much tax upon either time or patience. It is
specially important to bachelors, as it is the

4

means by which the unattached are kept in touch with the set or sets of society which they are privileged to enter. On returning to town after any continued absence, and on learning that his friends are in residence also, a bachelor should leave cards at the houses of those he has been in the habit of visiting, that they may know that he is available, and that he is desirous of remaining upon the visiting terms he has previously enjoyed. The cards, of which he should leave two, one for the lady and one for the gentleman of the house, should be of the standard shape and size, procurable of any stationer, with the name in the centre, preferably in plain script form. In the case of all commoners, the prefix Mr. should be used, and should not be omitted. Knights and Baronets use the prefix " Sir " but not the affix " Knt." or " Bart." An " Honourable " contents himself with Mr., but all holders of titles use them. Such affixes as K.C., M.P., D.L., or M.A., are not used, but military, naval, and clerical titles are used as prefixes. The address, the club, and, in the case of a military man, the name of the regiment, may also be given. Cards should not be left on too slight acquaintance, even after a formal introduction, and in the case of ladies, the bachelor should wait some intimation that his visit would be agreeable, on receiving which he should leave cards as soon as possible, one for the lady and one for her natural guardian—her husband, her father, or her mother, and this whether he is acquainted with them or not. An invitation to an entertainment is an indication that acquaintance is desired, and cards should be left after all entertainments, whether accepted or not. It is a sign that the person leaving them desires the continuation of the acquaintance. Many hostesses keep a record of cards left and calls made, and failure to observe the formality often causes omissions when guest-lists are revised. Bachelors should show this civility after entertainments given by other bachelors of slight acquaintance. The system of card leaving is an elaborate yet quite reasonable arrangement for enabling society to limit its own circles, and to say with perfect courtesy to those whom they may deem undesirable acquaintances, " Thus far shalt thou come and no farther." Among intimate friends rules are commonly relaxed.

Garden-Parties are of several kinds—town, country, afternoon, and evening. Town garden-parties are given in June and the following months, country garden-parties in August and September, after the close of the London season. The larger garden-parties take the form of open-air receptions, the smaller ones of "At-Homes." Except for those who take part in sports such as are often included in the programmes of country garden-parties, morning-dress is worn in the afternoon. Gentlemen wear evening-dress at evening garden-parties, but in deference to the English climate, considerable latitude is enjoyed by ladies. A garden-party which lasts from nine until twelve at night involves risks to ladies in evening-dress, which prudence forbids them to run, and fashion does not require. Smart morning-dress with a light wrap as an extra precaution is accepted. Gentlemen in evening-dress wear light overcoats for similar reasons.

Evening At-Homes, Receptions, and Parties are of several kinds, and each is ordered differently after its manner. Sometimes an evening party follows a dinner, at other times the dinner is omitted, and the arrangements include a supper. When preceded by a dinner, the invitations are to dinner, and it should be indicated that dinner will be followed by a "Reception" or an "At-Home." When the dinner is omitted, the word "Reception" or "At-Home" should be used, and "At-Home" cards should be used for invitations. When guests of special distinction are to be present, the term "To meet so-and-so" is included on the invitation, and when entertainment is intended, the word "Music" should be added. The word "Reception" is used when large and important gatherings are intended; the word "At-Home" when assemblies of more modest pretensions are proposed. There is an official air about the word "Reception" which to some extent characterises the function, and there is a social flavour about the word "At-Home" which makes in some measure its differentiation. Nevertheless there are "receptions" which are quite "warm" in more senses than one, and

there are " at-homes " which are both cold and
dull. The hour varies according to circumstances. In the country all hours are earlier
than in town, and in town the tendency is for
hours to get later and later. The hour of the
" reception " or the " at-home " is arranged so
that it may not interfere with the dinner which
precedes it, whether in the same house or
another, and as the dinner-hour is late, the hour
of assembling for the "reception" or the "at-
home" is correspondingly postponed. Official
"receptions" are commonly timed for 10.30
or 11 p.m., in private circles for ten o'clock or
even earlier, according to circumstances. As
a rule the reception following a dinner in the
same house is later than otherwise, and special
entertainment is not necessary; but when the
reception or " at-home " is to occupy the whole
evening, a more or less formal programme is
provided. Where the house admits of it, the
hostess receives her guests at the top of the
staircase, any time within an hour after the time
named on the invitation. The guests then pass
into the drawing-room, where they are welcomed by the host. The arrangements as to
"announcements" must be left in the hands
of the attendant appointed for the duty, and the
best advice one can give a novice is, keep your
eyes open, observe what others do, and "follow
my leader."

Conduct in the drawing-room is of course
determined by the nature of the programme
provided. Introductions which involve no
more than passing acquaintance are frequently
made by the hostess on her own initiative, as she
may think it necessary in order to make isolated
individuals feel " at home." Persons of distinction who have not previously met are usually
presented to each other. When solo music is
being rendered, silence should be observed, but
this does not apply to the performance of a
band when it is only intended to accompany
conversation. Much depends upon the size of
the gathering. A " crush " is often little more
than an opportunity for the display of the
Christian virtues, when the visitors have to
remember the " charity that hopeth all things,
beareth all things, and suffereth long, and is
kind "; and where it is absolutely necessary to

let tribulation work patience, and "patience have her perfect work." At comparatively small gatherings, to which the word "reception" does not apply, and the words "evening party" are even more applicable than the term "at-home" the programme may well include competitions and games in which a large proportion of those present may join, and with regard to which more is said under the heading of Entertainment (see p. 119), and Indoor Games for Adults, which are described on pp. 161-180. Light refreshments are commonly provided in an adjoining room. THE ORDER OF GOING IN TO SUPPER which is of the nature of a supper provided at a ball, is similar to that observed when proceeding to dinner. Precedence of rank is always observed as far as possible, and as far as the higher ranks are concerned this is not difficult. Royalty always goes first: a prince with the hostess in charge, and a princess in the care of the host. A separate table is provided for royal persons, at which they are joined by the host and hostess, and such other guests as they may wish to sup with. Apart from royalty, the host or hostess tells the principal gentlemen guests whom they wish them to take in to supper, and the remainder make their own selection and follow. When the dimensions of the supper-room are not equal to the accommodation of the whole party, the guests are served in relays. In such cases a musical programme should always be provided in the drawing-room, to entertain the guests who are waiting their turn. It is not necessary to return to the drawing-room after supper, nor to take formal leave of the host and hostess. CARDS should be left at the house for host and hostess within a week of a dinner, an "at-home" or a ball, and this rule obtains whether the person invited was able to accept the invitation or not. Men who wish their names to be kept on visiting-lists, must not neglect these apparently trifling formalities.

THE BALL.

> THERE's music in the gallery,
>   There's dancing in the hall,
> And the girl I love is moving
>   Like a goddess through the ball.

Amongst a score of rivals
   You're the fairest in the room,
But I like you better, Marion, Marion, Marion,
I like you better, Marion,
   Riding through the broom.

It was but yester morning—
   The vision haunts me still—
That we looked across the valley,
   As our horses rose the hill ;
And I bade you read my riddle,
   And I waited for my doom,
While the spell was on us, Marion, Marion, Marion,
The spell was on us, Marion,
   Riding through the broom.

The wild bird carolled freely,
   The May was dropping dew,
The day was like a day from heaven,
   From heaven, because of you ;
And on my heart there broke a light,
   Dispelling weeks of gloom,
While I whispered to you, Marion, Marion,
   Marion,
While I whispered to you, Marion,
   Riding through the broom,

" What is freer than the wild bird ?
   What is sweeter than the May ?
What is fresher than the morning,
   And brighter than the day ? "
In your eye came deeper lustre,
   On your cheek a softer bloom,
And I think you guessed it, Marion, Marion,
   Marion,
I think you guessed it, Marion,
   Riding through the broom.

And now they flutter round you,
   These insects of an hour,
And I must stand aloof and wait,
   And watch my cherished flower ;
I glory in her triumphs,
   And I grudge not her perfume,
But I love you best, my Marion, Marion, Marion,
I love you best, my Marion,
   Riding through the broom.

                    WHYTE-MELVILLE.

At a Ball.—In the opinion of the writer, it is as natural for a girl to dance as for a bird to sing. A ray of sunshine is sufficient to quicken a whole tree into song, and a strain of music is enough to stir the movement of as many twinkling feet. If this be so, it would seem little less than a duty incumbent upon men that they should acquire an art which is capable of giving so much pleasure to the opposite sex. But alas! it is also true that there probably is nothing in which we display more selfishness than in the pursuit of pleasure, and there is no room in the house in which this is more conspicuous than in the ball-room. Those who are not dancing men should not accept invitations to dances. To do so is to obtain whatever pleasure they acquire under false pretences. It is neither fair to the hostess nor to the other guests. For men to congregate at the buffet, or lounge about the corridors, while ladies are compelled to idleness for want of partners is to show a general discourtesy which cannot be justified. Too much attention to the few ladies who may be considered the more attractive, however gratifying to the ladies themselves—though it is not by any means always so—is a distinct rudeness to the others. To engage a lady for a dance, and not to join her until the dance is half over, is an outrage.

A "ball" is usually a big dance with an extended programme; a "dance" is commonly a "small-and-early." The hours stated on the invitation card may be taken as indicating the importance of the gathering. Regulations as to dress are the same for a ball as for a dinner-party or an evening "At-Home," except that the shoes best adapted for dancing should be worn. White gloves and ties are worn, and white waistcoats are admissible. Black ties are not taboo, but signs of mourning are out of place in scenes of gaiety. The ordinary regulations of evening-dress prevail. The guests are usually received by the hostess on the landing above the staircase, or at the entrance to the ball-room itself. Once "received," the gentleman should look round the room for any ladies with whom he may be acquainted, and fix up the earlier dances without delay. If he wishes to extend his list, his host and hostess will readily effect the necessary introductions. At large balls, private or public, stewards are always available for this duty. These introductions should be made and accepted for the purposes of dancing only, and must not be taken to justify after-acquaintance. The inscription of the name on the programme of a partner should in all cases be legible. It is due to both that one should know with whom one is dancing. At private dances and balls, friendship may sometimes grow apace. Love, courtship, and marriage have been known to follow one another with some rapidity; but it is due to the lady that in the earlier stages of friendship she should have every opportunity of terminating acquaintance if she desires to. At public balls more marked restraint is observed. In France a gentleman conducts his partner to a seat immediately after a dance, bows, and leaves her. He would consider it a rudeness to locate himself at her side. In England at private dances, and sometimes at public balls, there is no impropriety in offering refreshments; but with strangers this should be done differentially, and should not be unduly pressed. In the matter of refreshments *chaperones* should not be forgotten. The real acquisition at a dance is the man who will find at least some part of his pleasure in giving pleasure to others, and who will do his best to help his host and hostess to promote the happiness of all. Douglas Jerrold was once asked who the gentleman was at that moment dancing with his wife, when he replied, " I really don't know, I am sure; some member of the Royal Humane Society, I should think ! " No lady would of course like to be asked to dance from motives of charity, but humane members of society should really take care that there is no necessity for the reason given by a Chicago girl when asked to dance, " Wal, yes, I guess I will ! I reckon I'll take root if I sit here much longer."

Country Visits are usually made for specified terms, which are named in the invitations. This is much more satisfactory than the old indefiniteness, which often led to embarrassment. Invitations should be answered without delay, as otherwise, in the case of refusal, some other friend may miss or go short of invitation. Country life is in some respects more free than town life, but such forms as obtain must be observed. The hour of arrival should be notified in good time, that the guest may be met on arrival. On reaching the house the guest will be shown to his room and a servant will, if he wishes it, unpack his portmanteau, and dispose of his clothes in the wardrobe and chest of drawers provided for the purpose. The hours of meals will be made known to him, and it will be his first business to observe them.

As no two households are exactly alike, it will become the guest to take his bearings carefully, watch procedure, and adapt himself generally to the plans, tastes, and habits of his host and hostess. The visitor at a country house is admitted to the domestic circle with a freedom that does not obtain to the same extent in town. One may be on friendly and even intimate terms with people in London society, and yet often it is not until one has stayed with them at a country-house that one really gets to know them. The greater the freedom allowed the greater the necessity for self-restraint, and the more circumscribed the area of action the more need there is for scrupulous attention to all the delicate courtesies of refined life.

Out of doors the country affords the best opportunities for manly sport, and there is no physical exercise in which man can engage which is more full of the joy of life than a day in the saddle.

Now—Thorough the copse, where the fox is found,
And over the brook, at a mighty bound,
And over the high lands, and over the low,
O'er furrows, o'er meadows, the hunters go !

Away !—as a hawk flies full at its prey,
So flieth the hunter, away—away !
From the burst at the cover, till set of sun,
When the red fox dies and—the day is done !

Oh !—*what* delight can a mortal lack,
When he once is firm on his horse's back,
With his stirrups short, and his snaffle strong,
And the blast of the horn for his morning song ?

                                B. W. PROCTER.

4*

HALF AN HOUR BEFORE SUPPER.

" So she's here, your unknown Dulcinea—the
    lady you met on the train,
And you really believe she would know you
    if you were to meet her again ? "

" Of course," he replied, " she would know me ;
    there never was womankind yet
Forgot the effect she inspired. She excuses,
    but does not forget."

" Then you told her your love ? " asked the
    elder ; while the younger looked up with
    a smile :
" I sat by her side half an hour—what else was
    I doing the while ?

" What, sit by the side of a woman as fair as the
    sun in the sky,
And look somewhere else lest the dazzle flash
    back from your own to her eye ?

" No, I hold that the speech of the tongue be as
    frank and as bold as the look,
And I held up myself to herself—that was more
    than she got from her book.

" Young blood ! " laughed the elder ; " no
    doubt you are voicing the mode of to-day :
But then we old fogies at least gave the lady
    some chance for delay.

" There's my wife—(you must know)—we first
    met on the journey from Florence to Rome ;
It took me three weeks to discover who was she,
    and where was her home ;

" Three more to be duly presented ; three more
    ere I saw her again ;
And a year ere my romance *began* where yours
    ended that day on the train."

" Oh, that was the style of the stage-coach ;
    we travel to-day by express ;
Forty miles to the hour," he answered, " won't
    admit of a passion that's less."

"But what if you make a mistake?" quoth
    the elder. The younger half sighed.
"What happens when signals are wrong or
    switches misplaced?" he replied.

"Very well, I must bow to your wisdom," the
    elder returned, "but submit
Your chances of winning this woman your
    boldness has bettered no whit.

"Why, you do not at best know her name. And
    what if I try your ideal
With something, if not quite so fair, at least
    more *en règle* and real?

"Let me find you a partner. Nay, come, I
    insist—you shall follow—this way.
My dear, will you not add your grace to entreat
    Mr. Rapid to stay?

"My wife, Mr. Rapid—Eh, what? Why, he's
    gone—yet he said he would come.
How rude! I don't wonder, my dear, you are
    properly crimson and dumb?"

Bret Harte.

THE LATEST DECALOGUE.

Thou shalt have one God only; who
Would be at the expense of two?
No graven images may be
Worshipped, except the currency:
Swear not at all; for, for thy curse
Thine enemy is none the worse:
At church on Sunday to attend
Will serve to keep the world thy friend:
Honour thy parents; that is, all
From whom advancement may befall:
Thou shalt not kill; but need'st not strive
Officiously to keep alive:
Do not adultery commit;
Advantage rarely comes of it:
Thou shalt not steal; an empty feat,
When it's so lucrative to cheat:
Bear not false witness; let the lie
Have time on its own wings to fly:
Thou shalt not covet, but tradition
Approves all forms of competition.

A. H. Clough.

Tips.—The tipping of servants is a vexed question and one for which it is difficult to lay down rules. The feeling of hosts and guests alike is against the system, and the tendency is towards its discouragement. The modern man is to be congratulated that things are not so bad as they were at one time, and that there are signs of a still further amelioration of the visitor's lot in the matter of paying fines to servants for the privilege of visiting their masters. Pope had to refuse invitations to a great house unless they were accompanied by the wherewithal to satisfy the servants. Vulgar wealth is the real demoraliser and refined consideration suffers. Custom is still strong, and while it obtains must not be overlooked. Sums must vary with the standard of the household and the measure of the services which claim requital. To-day the gamekeeper expects five pounds for preserving at his master's expense the game the visitor is invited to shoot. The butler at a large establishment would lose his self-respect if he took anything less than gold. Silver suffices for the housemaid, unless the guest has made a prolonged stay, in which case he will not begrudge a smaller or larger gold coin. A riding man will, of course, tip the groom and the stable-boy, for which, as a rule, he will have received value for money. The coachman who facilitates the visitor's arrival and departure, and the valet who conveniences his stay, will both be sufficiently interested in his welfare to desire to drink his health or otherwise celebrate his visit. Except in the case of the gamekeeper and the butler, who are paid for their positions, the measure of extra service rendered may be taken to determine the amount which should be paid.

While deprecating the tipping system, there is quite room for a word or two upon the subject of civility to servants. All service faithfully and courteously rendered deserves recognition, and though it is not necessary always to express one's thanks verbally, there is a manner of accepting service which is more eloquent than words. It is those most dependent upon servants who show them the least courtesy, and the person who is polite only to those whom he regards as equals, parades his own ill-breeding.

THE TYRANNY OF THE TIP.

F. RAYMOND COULSON

(From " A Jester's Jingles," by permission)

WHEN first upon this earth I came,
And went to church to get my name,
 A noisy little rip,
The dame who put us in the pew
Received (I'm told they always do
 At christenings) a tip.

When budding sense its leaves uncurled
I blossomed out into the world,
 A slender little slip,
At quite an early age I found
The thing that makes the world go round
 Is everywhere a tip.

The gentleman who brought the coal ;
His friend who shot it down the hole ;
 The boy I'd like to whip,—
The butcher's boy who came each day ;
The duke who took the dust away ;
 They all required a tip.

Yea, these and many hundreds more
(To name them all would be a bore,
 And so the list I skip),
Vast hordes were ranged on every hand
To whom the custom of the land
 It was to give a tip.

And when I grew to man's estate—
'Twas hopeless to elude my fate—
 I fell within their grip,
And I became, as *you* have done,
Like every other mother's son,
 A victim of the tip.

The barber's " help " who cuts my chin,
The man who brings my dinner in,
 The steward on the ship,
The " boots," and six or seven swells
Of servants found at all hotels,
 They all expect a tip.

The porter—that confounded skunk
Who drops my bag, who tents my trunk—
 He has me on the hip,
One puts my luggage in the train,
Another takes it out again—
 They both exact a tip.

'Tis thus at every step in life,
Yea, even when I took a wife
 I felt their cruel nip ;
The parson and the parson's clerk
(The latter grabbed it like a shark)
 Received the usual tip.

And so where'er my steps I wend,
From the beginning to the end,
 My hand I have to dip
Within my pocket—why, the knave,
The very churl who digs my grave
 At last, will want a tip !

Such is my lot. I don't complain
(And if I did 'twould be in vain).
 But oh, with quivering lip
I ask of Fate, the fickle minx,
" Why is it no one ever thinks
 Of giving *me* a tip ? "

And lo ! next morning in the Strand,
I met a man who gripped my hand
 With fast and fervent grip.
It was my old acquaintance Jones.
Said he in confidential tones,
 " Now do you want a tip ? "

" Certes, 'twould be exceeding strange,
A very gratifying change,"
 Said I with smiling lip.
Quoth he, you'll take it ? " Why of course,"
Quoth I, whereat he named a horse,
 And *that* he called a " tip."

Alas ! I took it, to my cost ;
Five guineas was the sum I lost,
 Through Jones's " racing snip."
I knew that it was kindly meant,
But henceforth I am quite content.
 I do not want a tip.

COURTSHIP AND MARRIAGE.—Shakespeare tells us that " In the spring a young man's fancy lightly turns to thoughts of love," and doubtless the bright, fresh beauty of the optimistic season favours the union of hearts. But Cupid is fairly busy all the year round, and possibly actual statistics, could they be gathered, would show that other seasons are equally fruitful in inducing the serious consideration of matrimony. **The Proposal.**—The proverb has it, " none but the brave deserve the fair," and Sir Walter Raleigh said :

> " He either fears his fate too much
> Or his deserts are small,
> Who dares not put it to the touch
> To gain or lose it all."

To love a girl, and lack the courage to tell her so, though still occasional, is not the characteristic of modern youth, and while we would console the timid lover with the reflection that " love will find a way," we may add a word or two as to opportunities and methods which may encourage the fearful and facilitate the more courageous in entering upon that course which we are assured upon high authority " never did run smooth."

An offer of marriage is the highest compliment a man can pay to a woman, and as such should not be lightly undertaken and ungraciously received. Who lacks the courage necessary for a *viva-voce* proposal should fall back upon the use of the pen. The true lover will take care to show the utmost consideration for the feelings of the lady, and as a man of honour will only make such a proposal under circumstances which leave her quite free to accept or reject. The residence of the lady is the place which insures her the largest measure of independence, and she is entitled to such conditions when deciding upon so momentous an issue. If time is asked to consider the proposal, it should be granted cheerfully if with reluctance. Acceptance after consideration is a greater compliment than an immediate affirmative. Acceptance with a view to an engagement is usually followed by an interview with the lady's father or natural guardian. In some cases, especially where disparity of fortune exists, parents or guardians should be consulted first, and in these cases their decision should be accepted as final. This ordeal successfully passed, the accepted lover presents the lady with an engagement ring. These are made in great variety, and of all values, and as it is the first gift after betrothal a little extravagance is often condoned. Obviously this is a matter in which the lady's taste should be consulted. An engagement-ring is worn on the third finger of the left hand, until superseded in due course by the wedding-ring, when it commonly does duty as a keeper.

THE ENGAGEMENT.—It is not necessary to advertise an engagement. The ring tells its own story, and the word passes rapidly from mouth to mouth. The earliest opportunities should be taken for effecting introductions to the members of the two families. Dinner-parties in the first instance, and shorter or longer stays at the houses of each other's parents, often pleasantly accomplish this. The measure of liberty allowed by parents to engaged couples varies according to their ideas of strict propriety. In some cases the lady is always under the care of a *chaperon*. When this is so it is well to remember that a girl who is worth having at all is worth waiting for, and it should not be forgotten that the one who plays the part of gooseberry is often more to be commiserated than the young people who endure her supervision. There should of course be a desire on each side to contribute to the happiness of the other, and engaged couples should have every reasonable opportunity of so doing; but their devotion to each other should not be so complete and exclusive as to cause comment or to produce boredom. They have every right to enjoy their own society without intrusion, but when in company they have no right, by selfish isolation, to impair the enjoyment of others. Engagements are for longer or shorter periods, as determined by the ages and the positions of the principals. Young people are commonly engaged for two years. Shorter engagements are not uncommon, longer are not desirable. When from any cause it is felt wise to terminate an engagement, it is well not to delay the inevitable. The lady has the right of initiative, but in either case correspondence is the best means. When the engagement is broken off all presents are returned, and if either party feels aggrieved, it is best to forgive and forget.

WEDDINGS.—A wedding without a hitch is something of a rarity, albeit the occasion is one upon which it is desirable that everything should run as smoothly as possible. "There is nothing certain but the unforeseen," and the unexpected is an all-inclusive possibility. There are so many details which need arrangement, that it is quite easy to omit some necessary provision. The bridegroom, who is our chief concern here, has perhaps less to think of than some others and yet he has some important duties to discharge, and as he is for the whole day under the fierce light of observation, it is due to the bride as well as to himself that he should be in appearance and deportment above reproach. It is the bridegroom's duty to arrange for the marriage ceremony, of course in consultation with the bride and the responsible members of her family, as to time and place. Early-morning weddings are now less common than formerly: from two to three o'clock in the afternoon is the most popular hour. Marriages may be contracted in church by special licence, by licence, or after the publication of banns. **Marriage by special licence** is a costly matter. Licences are issued by the Archbishop of Canterbury on application at the Vicar-General's Office, Doctors' Commons, when sufficiently special reasons are given to satisfy him of the necessity or desirability. The cost is about £30. **An ordinary licence** can be obtained through the same office at a cost of £2, including fees and stamps. These licences are operative in any parish in which either of the contracting parties has resided for not less than fifteen days prior to the application, and are available for any church in the same. The cost of licences obtained through clerical surrogates in country districts differs with the diocese, but only to the extent of a few shillings. **Marriage by " banns "** is the more popular form ; perhaps its greater publicity adds to its piquancy. The fifteen days' residence before the banns are published is essential in these cases, and the banns must be published in both parishes. After the banns have been published at intervals of a week, three times consecutively, the marriage can take place. Fees to clergymen vary according to the position of the parties concerned. Any sum from one guinea upwards may be given. A smaller fee is always expected by and given to the clerk. **Marriages by the Registrar** require three weeks' notice, which must be given to the Registrar, who will cause the names of the contracting parties to be posted in his office for that period. The fees of the Registrar are fixed and small. Other conditions having been fulfilled, one day's notice is sufficient for marriage by licence at a registry office. **The church wedding** is the most popular, the office of the Registrar not lending itself to the traditions of matrimony, and not being suitable for the display which from time immemorial has been associated with the ceremony. The great majority of people are married but once in a lifetime, and it is a far better feeling than mere vanity which prompts a bride and bridegroom to desire a pretty wedding. It is a higher motive still which leads them to seek its solemnisation in a place of worship. It is the **bridegroom's duty** to provide the wedding-ring, the bride's bouquet, bouquets for the bridesmaids, and where means allow, presents for each. These should be sent to the house of their recipients the night previous to an early wedding, or on the morning of a later one. He provides his own carriage, in which he conveys his bride from the church to the reception after the wedding, and from the reception to the railway station when they go for their honeymoon. The coming of the motor has somewhat altered the order of this going, as some couples are thereby rendered independent of railway travelling. The bridegroom should be at the church in good time, as it is unpardonable to keep the bride waiting, and anything slovenly detracts from the smartness of a wedding. Ten minutes prior to the hour fixed leaves a reasonable margin. He may walk or ride as he pleases, but in either case should be accompanied by the friend who has undertaken the duties of groomsman. His dress should be a silk hat, a black-frock coat, a black or white waistcoat, a white tie and white gloves. If he wears a flower, it should be white and backed by maiden-

hair fern. A lavender tie with gloves and
trousers to match are sometimes worn, but
pronounced colours should be avoided. On
reaching the church the bridegroom should
proceed as far as the chancel steps, where the
first part of the ceremony takes place, and take
up his position on the right-hand side. Here
he awaits, in company with the groomsman, the
arrival of the bride. In the meantime the
bridesmaids have assembled in the vestibule,
and on the bride's arrival follow her and her
father up the aisle. On the approach of the
bride the bridegroom moves towards the
centre of the chancel steps and takes his place
on her right hand, the groomsman a step to the
rear at his right hand, and the bridesmaids forming a rearguard for the bride. From this point
the progress is plain sailing. The bridegroom
is in calm waters, and the pilot will see him safely
through. On the conclusion of the ceremony
the wedded couple follow the clergyman to the
vestry, the wife on her husband's left arm.
The formalities of the vestry need not be de-
cribed ; but, these over, the bridegroom again
offers his left arm to the bride and they return
through the church to their carriage. **The
groomsman** should be chosen with care, as he
has it in his power to a large extent to make
or mar the proceedings. The personal attendant of the bridegroom, it is his duty to see
that nothing is wanting to ensure the easy
progress of the ceremony. He has to make
sure that the ring is ready for its important
part, and the custody of the bridegroom's hat
is commonly his care. The gallant of the
chief bridesmaid, he leads her into the vestry
in the wake of the happy pair, and after the
formalities and the payment of all fees, having
seen to the departure of the bride and bridegroom
in the first carriage, the bride's mother and the
bridegroom's father in the second, and the
bride's father and the bridegroom's mother in
the third, and having arranged escorts for the
other bridesmaids, who are to follow, he accom-
panies the chief bridesmaid in the fourth carriage,
and is then ready to take up his duties in promoting the gaiety of the reception. **Speeches**
are at a discount at modern weddings, but there
are one or two which should never be omitted.

That of the bride and bridegroom should be entrusted to the speaker most likely to do it justice, and it should never be treated as a frivolous matter. When the clergyman is a guest the duty is often discharged by him. The bridegroom's duty is then to respond for himself and his bride, and sometimes it is to be feared that although the duty is very simple, and but few words need be said, it is on this that for the first time the wife sometimes very nearly feels just a little bit ashamed of her husband. To thank the proposer for the kind things said and wishes expressed, and the company for the heartiness of their response ought to be a simple and easy task, and to finish up by proposing the health of the bridesmaids and expressing the hope that they will all soon be brides, and to couple this toast with the name of the groomsman ought not to involve a moment's hesitation. The parents of the bride and bridegroom may be proposed together and responded to by each, or the two fathers may divide the proposal and response. **At receptions** light refreshments are handed round, and the gentlemen wait upon the ladies, the toasts being drunk at a convenient interval. **At a breakfast or luncheon** the bride and bridegroom occupy the chief seats, the bridegroom's mother and the bride's father on the left of the bride, and the bride's mother and the bridegroom's father on the bridegroom's right. The groomsman and the bridesmaids are the next in order of importance, and often occupy seats facing the happy pair. At the close of the meal the speeches are made and the ceremony of cutting the cake takes place, after which, as a rule, preparations are made for departure for the honeymoon. While the bride is 'tiring, the bridegroom, whose preparations are of a much simpler character, should, if he has time to spare, wait her readiness in the hall, there to experience a sweet and hearty send-off to the sea or the blue hills far away. As a rule the guests do not remain long after the departure of the bride and bridegroom, and unless there is an evening reception the proceedings close. (For speeches, see pp. 63-67.)

THE COURTSHIP OF THE FUTURE.

(A Prevision.)

(A.D. 2876.)

He.

"What is a kiss ?"—Why, long ago,
  When pairs, as we, a-wooing sat,
They used to put their four lips . . . so . . .
  And make a chirping noise . . . like that.
And, strange to say, the fools were pleased ;
  A little went a long .way then,
A cheek lip-grazed, a finger squeezed,
  Was rapture to those ancient men.

Ah, not for us the timid course
  Of those old-fashioned bill-and-cooers !
One unit of our psychic force
  Had squelched a thousand antique wooers.
For us the god his chalice dips
  In fountains fiercer, deeper, dearer,
Than purling confluence of lips
  That meet, but bring the souls no nearer.

Well ; 'twas but poverty at worst ;
  Poor beggars, how could they be choosers !
Not yet upon the world had burst
  Our Patent Mutual Blood Transfusers.
Not yet had science caught the clue
  To joy self-doubting,—squaring,—cubing,—
Nor taught to draw the whole soul through
  A foot of gutta-percha tubing.

Come, Lulu, bare the pearly arm ;—
  Now, where the subtle blue shows keenest,
I hang the duplex, snake-like charm
  (The latest, by a new machinist).
And see, in turn above my.wrist,
  I fix the blood-compelling conduits. . . .
Ah, this is what the old world missed,
  For all the lore of all its pundits !

I turn the tap—I touch the spring—
  Hush, Lulu, hush ! our lives are blending.
(This new escapement's quite the thing,
  And very well worth recommending.)
Oh, circuit of commingling bliss !
  Oh, bliss of mingling circulation !
True love alone can merge like this
  In one continuous pulsation.

Your swift life fills me through and through :
  I wouldn't call the Queen my mother :
Now you are I and I am you,
  And each of us is one another.
Reciprocally influent
  The wedded love-tide flows between us :—
Ah, this is what the old fables meant,
  For surely, love, our love is venous !

Now, now, your inmost life I know !
  How nobler far than mine, and grander ;
For through *my* breast *your* feelings flow,
  And through my brain your thoughts meander.
I feel a rush of high desires,
  With sweet domestic uses blending,
As now I think of angel-choirs,
  And now of stockings heaped for mending.

And see—myself ! in light enshrined !
  An aureole my hat replacing !
Now, amorous yearnings half-defined,
  With prudish scruples interlacing.
Next, cloudlike, floats a snowy veil,
  And—heavens above us !—what a trous-
     seau ! . . .
Come, Lulu, give me tale for tale ;
  I'll keep transfusing till you do so.

She.

Oh, love, this never *can* be you !
  The stream flows turbid, melancholic ;
And heavy vapours dull me through,
  Dashed with a something alcoholic,
The elective forces shrink apart,
  No answering raptures thrill and quicken ;
Strange feelings curdle at my heart,
  And in my veins vile memories thicken.

I feel an alien life in mine !
  It isn't I ! It isn't you, sir !
This is the mood of Caroline !
  Oh, don't tell *me* ! I know the brew, sir !
Nay, nay,—it isn't " the machine " !
  This isn't you—this isn't I, sir !
It's the old story—you have been
  Transfusing elsewhere on the sly, sir !

From the Poetical Works of Brunton Stephens by permission
of Messrs. Angus & Robertson, Sydney.

ENTERTAINMENT

In making up their lists of guests for social functions hosts and hostesses from time immemorial have aimed at gathering together those who will not only be mutually agreeable in association but who will also to some extent contribute to the entertainment of each other, and from the good old days when " Little Tom Tucker sang for his supper " musicians, actors, elocutionists, and conjurors have had many opportunities of paying for hospitality with talent. So long as amateurs are relied upon for this service no one has any right to complain, provided no one is pressed beyond convenience. All guests are invited for the sake of some pleasure they will give to the host or hostess, and the form in which they give the pleasure only differs in kind. The host who spreads his table and bids his guests to the enjoyment of the best he can provide has surely a right to expect them to make what return they can by contributing to the feast of reason and the flow of soul which follow, and it should surely be the desire of those best qualified to do so, to aid the host and hostess in the general entertainment. Of course it is bad taste to tax a guest to the impairing of his own enjoyment by making him the servant of the whole company, at the piano or in any other way, and it is more than bad taste to impose upon the generosity of professionals whose talents have a market value and who should be paid for their services at the market price. Hosts and hostesses who are not to the manner born have been known to presume upon the least possible acquaintance to ask professionals to give their professional services without any thought of offering them a pecuniary equivalent. There is no more reason in asking a professional singer whose fee is ten guineas to sing at a social function for nothing than there would be to ask a fashionable tailor to make a dress-suit to be

worn on the same occasion for the same return;
and yet successful business men will sometimes,
ignoring the capital sunk in professional training
and the labour spent on the acquisition of
artistic proficiency, coolly ask high-class professionals to make them a present of what is
really so much money in kind.

Some amusing stories are told of the way
in which famous professionals have dealt with
this kind of treatment. Some years ago there
was a favourite English prima donna, Miss
Paton, who married a tenor singer named
Wood and went to reside in America. Having
lived some time in Philadelphia, the lady was
invited to a party given by an American citizen,
who had become suddenly rich, and whose
wife used to give gay parties. They were
very vulgar people, and Mrs. Wood politely
declined the invitation; but nothing would
satisfy the citizen's lady but that Mrs. Wood
must appear, as she had announced that she
expected her in order to give *éclat* to her party.
So Mr. and Mrs. Wood reluctantly went. When
the entertainments of the evening were fairly
commenced, and several of the company had
sung, the hostess pressed Mrs. Wood to go
to the piano and sing, which she declined to
do on the ground of fatigue. The astonishment
created by Mrs. Wood's refusal to oblige her
friends was evinced by the hostess with a
fixed stare; at length she broke out with—
"What, not sing, Mrs. Wood? Why, it was for
this I invited you to my party." "Oh!"
replied Mrs. Wood, "I was not aware that you
invited me professionally, but since such was
your intention, I shall of course sing at once."
So Mrs. Wood seated herself at the piano,
and sang most delightfully everything that her
hostess and friends asked for, to the entire
gratification of all present. On the following
day, however, when the host and hostess were
counting up the cost of their entertainment
(for rich as they were they had not lost their
former regard for economy), to their astonishment and consternation there came in a demand
from Mr. Wood for one hundred dollars for
"Mrs. Wood's professional services" at their
party the preceding evening, accompanied by
a note couched in terms that made it quite

certain that the demand would be insisted on.
However much they were mortified by this
unexpected demand, they deemed it most
prudent to pay it, and hold their tongues.

A more dramatic protest, and one less likely
to be forgotten, was made by Sothern on one
occasion when visiting Liverpool to play his
famous part in *David Garrick* Invited to dine
and sup with the officers of a regiment then
stationed at the great port, and knowing full
well that he was only invited for the entertainment he was expected to afford, he determined to give one of his most famous dramatic
scenes, and so reproduced the scene from
David Garrick in which he represented a
drunken man at a dinner-table, to the discomfort of the guests and the destruction of
much theatrical " property." Following the
lines adopted on the stage with so much success,
he dragged off the tablecloth and scattered
with disastrous effect the cherished service of
china, glass, and plate, of which the regiment
were so proud. It was a rather vigorous protest,
but Sothern was an inveterate practical
joker, and this was one of his most costly
practical jokes. That was an officers' mess
which will not be soon forgotten.

Fischer, the famous oboe player, once gave
a very neat answer to a certain noble lord
who invited him to supper, adding the remark :
" Of course you will bring your oboe with
you." " Thank you, my lord," said the
musician, " my oboe never sups."

It is, of course, a matter for individual hosts
to determine, but as a rule it will be found best
either to engage **professionals** to provide *all*
the entertainment or to depend upon **amateurs**
for the whole programme, except, perhaps,
for a professional pianist—the demands made
by that position being more than it is fair to
make of a guest. If professionals are engaged,
the host is more certain of his programme,
and he is saved much trouble and arrangement.
But the presence of professionals is apt to
add to the stiffness and formality of the proceedings, and where the available amateur
talent is of a sufficiently high standard the
quality of the entertainment can be maintained
without any sacrifice of social freedom. The

mixing of amateurs and professionals is not always fair to the amateur, and has been known to give rise to unpleasant feelings. At the same time, as much amateur talent as may be available, with some professional skill in reserve, inspires the host and hostess with confidence, and has, times out of number, worked well.

While it is the duty of those able to contribute to the enjoyment of their fellow-guests to do so, and to do so without fuss—for fuss is always vulgar—it is equally the duty of those lacking qualification for such service to remain in the obscurity they are so much better fitted to adorn. The audience is just as necessary to the pleasure of the performer as the performer is to the pleasure of the audience, and a good listener contributes no small share to the success of a good performance. Both are necessary to a successful programme. If each of us were only content to play the part for which we are best qualified, we should save ourselves and others many disappointments.

The Duty of Silence is not always observed and it is much to be regretted that it should still be necessary to protest against the bad taste shown by people—women especially—in carrying on a conversation while music is being performed. It is an insult to the performer, and it is an affront to the host at whose request the performance is given. It is just as rude to show indifference to the entertainment arranged by the host as it would be to show indifference to the viands provided by him.

A famous French tenor is said to have been so much annoyed by the conversation which was carried on during his first song at a social function at which he had been engaged to sing, that he immediately left the house, and on the following day returned his fee, plus an amount as compensation for having interrupted the conversation of the guests.

Music is the most simple and popular form of entertainment available for social gatherings, and it is a quite indispensable element of public rejoicing. It is as difficult to imagine a social function without chamber-music as it is a public procession without flags flying and banners waving, without the music of the trumpet and the drum. A world without music is unimaginable;

and with full sympathy for the afflicted, few of us would care to inhabit a world of deaf-mutes. The writer once attended a religious service at which the prayers, the reading of the scriptures, the sermon, and even the hymns were rendered by the fingers. It was a service he will never forget, and probably novelty did something to fix it on his memory; but he is free to admit that it was far more impressive than many a service of the ordinary kind which he has attended since. None the less, Quakers' meetings, and others of the kind, are properly regarded as lacking elements of popularity.

But as we have already said, music is the most popular and easily available form of entertainment for social gatherings. The facilities afforded for the study of music in London and in other great civic centres have done much to raise the standard of both professional and amateur performances, and it would now surely be impossible to assemble a gathering having any pretensions to culture, in which there would not be musicians in sufficient number and variety to provide an excellent programme of high-class vocal and instrumental music. As a rule, the difficulty does not lie in lack of material so much as in the want of means of acquiring a sufficient knowledge of the nature and quality of the materials available, to enable the master of the ceremonies to make the best possible use of it. If ladies and gentlemen would only send on their music-cases beforehand, that the host, or some one acting for him, might go through them and make judicious selections, many useless repetitions and much undeserved *ennui* might be avoided, and a more artistic unity might be secured. At least it would enable the host to adopt the editorial process and formula, " Declined with thanks." That hosts are sometimes unduly troubled, not only by mediocrity which desires prominence, but also by talent which affects obscurity, is of course true. In the one case the offender forgets that obtrusiveness is an offence against good taste wherever it is shown, and in the other that it is the duty of the guest to do all that lies in his power to help his host in the entertainment of the other guests. Unfortunately genius is always modest, and it is often the reticence of the most able that compels a host to fall back upon the least fit. Mr. Cholmondely Pennell's *Musical Undertones* in "From Grave to Gay" gives humorous expression to the woes of a distracted M.C. under commonly recurring circumstances.

> "Herr Bellows, won't you sing?
> (Or rather won't you roar?)—
> I should like so to accompany you
> (As far as the street door.) . . .

> "Miss Squeals will take her part
> In that charming duet by Meyer,
> With Signor Buffo? (that's two at a go,
> I wish I could do them in 'choir'!)

> "Lord Whooper sings, I know?
> (Too well! and always flat)—
> What an exquisite air—(for a dirge on the stair
> Assisted by the cat!) . . .

> "Shan't we hear *your* voice, madame?
> (Be thanked! she's a cold in the head)—
> Pity our loss—(what a fool I was!
> She's going to 'play instead.') . . .

> "'Encore?' (oh, I can't stand this—
> They're going it 'hammer and tongs'—
> Confound them all! I'll get out in the hall
> And leather away at the gongs!)"
> 　　　　　　　(*By permission of Messrs. Longmans.*)

The subject of **Elocution** is too lengthy for treatment here, and the writer can only therefore refer the reader to his article on the "Rationale of Elocution" in his "New Standard Elocutionist," published by Messrs. Hutchinson & Co., London. This treats of deportment, action, delivery, pitch, articulation, pronunciation, inflection, emphasis, modulation, pause and pace, passion and dramatic force. An article on the physiology of the vocal organs, by Lennox Brown, F.R.C.S., and one by Clifford Harrison on "Musical Accompaniments to Recitation" are also included in that volume. A number of pieces suitable for recitation are included in this book.

Ventriloquism is a form of entertainment which, well executed, never fails to fascinate. The first requirement of the art is a natural power of mimicry. A good mimic, with a sympathetic voice, has only to practise to become a good ventriloquist. The phrase commonly used, "throwing the voice," is one which throws the inquirer off the scent, and this is probably its purpose. No one can throw his voice, but a good mimic can imitate where he is, sounds as they would appear if coming from a distance.

This has only to be done without any perceptible movement of the lips to make the illusion complete. To put it in a sentence, the ventriloquist's art is that of employing the perspective of acoustics to deceive the ear as the scene-painter employs the perspective of his peculiar art to deceive the eye. The performer occupies a platform or a seat at the fireside, and his imitations are of voices as they would sound if they came through a partition from the rear of the stage, from the roof above, or from the cellar below, or in the case of the drawing-room performance, from the chimney, or from an adjoining conservatory. He can make the audience in the front row think that the sounds he makes come from the back of the room, and he can make the people at the back of the room think that the sounds come from the back of the stage, but he cannot make the people in the back of the room think that the sounds come from among themselves. Many of the pranks played by the famous Valentine Vox are quite possible in practice ; others can only be performed between the covers of a book. A mere exhibition of mimicry is always interesting, and the way in which a good mimic can imitate the sounds made by a carpenter's tools—the plane, the saw, etc., etc., the sounds made by animals and birds, dogs, cats, horses, donkeys, pigs, cocks, hens, ducks, geese, etc. etc., of themselves will keep a party of children amused for a long time. **The Doll** used by professional ventriloquists, and many who have no claim to natural powers of mimicry, helps to eke out a performance which would often enough be tame indeed if the performer were compelled to rely upon real ventriloquial skill. The clever patter which many performers put together is in the highest degree amusing, albeit the entertainment is one that cannot properly be described as ventriloquial. All that is necessary in this case is the ability to counterfeit the single voice that represents the doll, and to carry on the part of the conversation attributed to the doll without showing any movement of the lips. This latter is much easier than it appears. There are only a few letters which cannot be sounded without a movement of the lips, and if words using these letters are avoided in the patter prepared and learnt by heart beforehand, any ordinary person can perform this part of the entertainment without difficulty. The letter sounds to be avoided are B, F, M, P, V, W, and Y. Such words as bibacious, fulfil, momentous, peripatetic, vivacity, westward, and other words which require V to be sounded broadly. It need hardly be said that whatever the patter may be it should be entirely free from vulgarity. Vulgarity is not fit for any place, and it is little less than blasphemy in a home of culture. **In Burlesque.**—A very amusing impromptu entertainment may be got up by two confederates imitating a ventriloquist and his doll. In this case the one who acts the part of the doll wears a lady's cap, collar, and blouse, and sits behind a narrow table, the drapery of which obscures the rest of his costume. Leaning forward, he presents the appearance of a bust of a figure resting on the table. A veil falling over the shoulders conceals the hand of the professor, which, placed at the back of the head, manipulates it after the manner of a performer dealing with the real thing. With the other hand the professor will close the mouth of the figure occasionally, and turn the chin towards himself as he is wont to do in an ordinary performance. The patter may be quite the usual thing, but the climax is reached when the professor having called in vain to the supposed man on the roof or in the cellar, the doll says, "Mr. Johnson, you're a fraud," rises, and leaves the hall.

Conjuring is a form of entertainment which requires more care and study than the average amateur can afford to give to a mere amusement, and frequently more tedious preparation than he cares to make for an entertainment which, however wonderful to the audience, is entirely without novelty to himself. Tricks requiring mechanical appliances also include storage and carriage, to say nothing of initial cost, hence the rôle of the conjurer who gives entertainments is generally left to the professional. An amateur desirous of rivalling professional variety cannot do better than pay a visit to one of the well-known houses that deal in magic and mystery, where they can purchase all sorts of contrivances for deceiving the eye, with full instructions for their effective use. Those who may be content to amuse small circles at a dinner-table or in a drawing-room with the dexterous manipulation of handkerchiefs, cards, coins, watches, matches, and other properties always available on such occasions, may learn many without much trouble from books, whose name is legion, and which can be purchased at very little cost. Firms like those of Messrs. Hamley & Co. may be consulted with regard to apparatus, and books like those of Professor Hoffman, Mr. Devant, and other famous conjurers may be trusted to provide vast stores of informative material for suggestive experiment. Sleight-of-hand, in which "the quickness of the hand deceives the eye," requires much practice with naturally muscular and mobile hands if palming—which enters so largely into its methods—is to attain expert efficiency. Conjuring entertainments should not be unduly prolonged, and great care should be taken to insure variety. Too many tricks more or less alike become very monotonous, and the conjurer needs to remember that while he is at liberty to use as much patter as may be necessary to conceal his thoughts, brevity is still the soul of wit.

Palmistry is a profession which enjoys, or otherwise, the unique experience of being practised as a science and punished as a crime. If a lady with a high-sounding name, which does not belong to her, rents an expensive flat at the West End of London, and charges high prices to blasé wealth, the law smiles complacently and the policeman "winks the other eye"; if a poor old woman of Romany origin and habit who lives in a slum ventures for a few coppers to tell a servant girl that "the lines have fallen to her in pleasant (or other) places," she is "a danger to society," and must be dealt with by a stipendiary. Should the lady with the high-sounding name, for which she has no licence, remove the practice of her profession to some country district she will come under the jurisdiction of "the great unpaid," where she may learn that urban and suburban justice are two different things, for here, as Punch once put it,

> "You buy your justice at the dearest rate
> Of the non-paid noodle, the magistrate."

But whether a science or a fraud when tested by monetary payment or judged by judicial standards, there can be no doubt that it is often a fashionable amusement, and if pretence, be not carried too far, may even serve a useful purpose. In these frivolous days, anything which makes people think does some good, and in palmistry, as in many other things, the more or less of it will depend upon the spirit and skill of the operator. Responsibility attaches to all influence, and no one is justified in lightly treating important subjects which are liable to be taken too seriously in this connection. Books on palmistry abound, and lessons can easily be obtained, and as it is impossible within the limits of these pages to treat it thoroughly, we must content ourselves with these few observations, and with pointing out that the opportunity palmistry affords for holding delicate hands and pouring "soft nothings," seasoned by sweet somethings, into dainty ears, is one that need not be taboo to a diner-out.

Phrenology has made great progress in scientific as well as popular recognition in recent years, and without attempting to appraise its value from either point of view, it will suffice to say here that the more we consider natural phenomena the more we become convinced that everything means something, and that accepted interpretations are not always exact or comprehensive. Investigation has much to discover and experience a great deal to adjust before any one can afford to be dogmatic. Phrenology as practised by well-known accredited professors is a serious study, and some of them wisely refuse to treat it as an amusement. None the less, examples given in a drawing-room, whether by professionals or amateurs, always excite intelligent interest, and may often give a great deal of useful pleasure without any derogation to its more serious practice. Here again we are obliged, from want of space, to refer the reader to books devoted entirely to the subject, or to private tuition, which need not be far to seek. That delineations should always be made with discretion, and that all observations should be kindly, and in good taste, goes without saying.

Tableaux, to be all that they may be, should be forecast and rehearsed. The impromptu effort may be amusing, and need not be eliminated from the resources of rough-and-ready entertainment, but well-prepared living pictures may be made so artistic that it is a pity to spoil them for want of pre-arrangement, thought, and care. A very wide range of subjects may be selected from, but a good plan is to choose a famous picture, an historic incident, or a scene from a standard poem or novel, and reproduce it with as much fidelity to life as may be possible under the circumstances. Indoor scenes are more easily arranged for indoor entertainment, and classical subjects afford excellent opportunities for graceful pose. Tableaux are sometimes taboo on account of expense. A little ingenuity may, however, often minimise cost, and moderate mechanical skill easily heighten effect. For instance, marble terraces and tessellated floors may be very cheaply represented by common wall-papers, and art muslins, serges, sateens, chintzes, cretonnes, and casement cloths form effective and inexpensive drapery.

PERVERTED PROVERBS.

Once hit twice fly.

Necessity is the mother of prevention.

Children should be cream and not curd.

A switch in time saves crime.

What can't be cured must be insured.

All things come round to him who pays the freight.

It's an ill mind that owes nobody any good.

One good turn desires another opportunity.

A man is known by the company he promotes.

Where there's a will there's a way—for the lawyer.

Experience makes fools wise in their own conceit.

Eat to live but do not live to eat humble pie.

Never cry over spilt milk unless you're a cowherd.

Facts are stubborn things, and most women are facts.

If stands stiff for all the curl over its forehead.

Two heads are better than one under the mistletoe.

A. H. M.

HUMOROUS VERSE FOR RECITATION.

THE TENDER HEART.—HELEN GREY CONE.

SHE gazed upon the burnished brace
   Of partridges he showed with pride ;
Angelic grief was in her face ;
   " How *could* you do it, dear ? " she sighed.
" The poor, pathetic, moveless wings !
   The songs all hushed—oh, cruel shame ! "
Said he, " The partridge never sings."
   Said she, " The sin is just the same.

" You men are savage through and through.
   A boy is always bringing in
Some string of birds' eggs, white or blue,
   Or butterfly upon a pin.
The angle-worm in anguish dies,
   Impaled, the pretty trout to tease—— "
" My own, I fish for trout with flies—— "
   " Don't wander from the question, please !

She quoted Burns's " Wounded Hare,"
   And certain burning lines of Blake's,
And Ruskin on the fowls of air,
   And Coleridge on the water-snakes.
At Emerson's " Forbearance " he
   Began to feel his will benumbed ;
At Browning's " Donald " utterly
   His soul surrendered and succumbed.

" Oh, gentlest of all gentle girls,"
   He thought, " beneath the blessèd sun ! "
He saw her lashes hung with pearls,
   And swore to give away his gun.
She smiled to find her point was gained,
   And went, with happy parting words
(He subsequently ascertained),
   To trim her hat with humming-birds.

THE ARTISTS.—EVA L. OGDEN.

SHE was rich and of high degree ;
A poor and unknown artist he.
" Paint me," she said, " a view of the sea."
So he painted the sea as it looked the day
That Aphrodite arose from its spray ;

And it broke, as she gazed in its face the while
Into its soulless, dimpled smile.

"What a pokey, stupid picture," said she;
"I don't believe he *can* paint the sea!"

Then he painted a raging, tossing sea,
Storming, with fierce and sudden shock,
Wild cries, and writhing tongues of foam,
A towering, mighty fastness rock.
In its sides above those leaping crests
The thronging sea-birds built their nests.

"What a disagreeable daub," said she;
"Why it isn't anything like the sea!"

Then he painted a stretch of hot, brown sand,
With a big hotel on either hand,
And a handsome pavilion for the band,—
Not a sign of the water to be seen
Except one faint little streak of green.

"What a perfectly exquisite picture," said she;
"It's the very *image* of the sea!"

THE TURTLE-DOVES.

THEY sat there in the gloaming; the night
    breeze murmured by,
Its melody a cadence half-laden with a sigh.
She turned and eyed him fondly, then gently,
    softly, said:
"The years have left their record upon your
    snowy head,
But still I can't forget them, those days so bright
    and blue,
When you were 'lovey-dovey' and I was
    'ootsey-oo.'"

The moon hung low; the moonbeams came
    mellow from afar;
Across the hazy distance there gleamed the
    evening star.
The hour had made her tender, had called to
    mind the past.
"Ah!"—tremblingly she breathed it—"if those
    young days could last!
They still come trooping to me, those days so
    glad and true,
When you were 'lovey-dovey' and I was
    'ootsey-oo.'"

Uneasily he twisted upon his rocking-chair.
" Do you recall," she asked him, " those days so
　　sweet and fair ?
Do you remember, darling, how dear it seemed
　　to you
When I said ' lovey-dovey ' and you said
　　' ootsey-oo ' ? "
He found his voice that moment, and ootsey-oo
　　was jarred—
" No, I never can forget them ; but I've tried
　　to jolly hard."

Judge.

OFFICIAL.

" You can decorate your office with a thousand
　　gilded signs,
And have upholstered furniture in quaint,
　　antique designs ;
Have the latest patent telephone where you can
　　yell ' Hello ! '
But," said she, " I've just made up my mind
　　that typewriter must go."

" You can stay down at the office, as you have
　　done, after hours ;
And, if you're partial to bouquets, I'll furnish
　　you with flowers,
You can spring the old club story when you come
　　home late, you know,
But, remember, I've made up my mind that
　　typewriter must go."

" You can let your clerks have holidays to see
　　a game of ball,
The office boy can leave at noon or not show up
　　at all.
But—what is this upon your coat ? It isn't
　　mine, I know.
I think I know a thing or two—that typewriter
　　must go."

THE WHEEL OF FATE.

(With Acknowledgments to Omar Khayyám)

[It is suggested that, in view of the dangers of our motor-
ridden roads, Insurance Companies might now sell tickets at
the pavement edge.]

O THOU whose eyes like beams of Morning Light
Illume my soul : look up ! the skies are bright ;
　　Let us go forth and drink the Joy of Spring,
For biting Winter may return To-night !

Come, seek thy Bliss, the Dearest and the Best
From out the wondrous Windows of the West—
　　The Hat and Costume of thy Heart's Desire,
And—since I love Thee—I will do the rest.

Ah, Love, yet ere we press with eager feet
Those ways, the destined Hat and Garb to greet,
　　Discretion calls, " Insure Her life and Thine,
For there are Motorists in every Street ! "

Swift Peril lurks Behind us and Before,
And we that sally smiling to the Store
　　May fall beneath the Whirling Wheel of Fate
Whence Dogs, and Fowls, and Men arise no more.

For I remember pausing Yesterday
Where dead the Bird of Spring—poor chicken !
　　lay :
　　And, lo, a Voice within the Tavern cried,
" A cursèd Motorist hath passed this Way ! "

The Wheel no question makes of Eyes or Nose,
But Here or There, as strikes the Chauffeur,
　　goes,
　　And ere the Pale Pedestrian has reached
The Kerb he sought his Day has met its Close.

A moment's halt ; Thy foot or Mine misplaced
Amid this mesh of traffic interlaced,
　　And—no more Hats for Thee ! And no more
　　Spring,
And no more days for Kissing.　Oh, make haste !

A merchant at the kerb vends Tickets.　See !
Insurance policies for Thee and Me.
　　A Thousand Pounds for Some one if we die—
For Some one who is neither Me nor Thee !

Ah, my Beloved, we know to our Despair
Insurance cannot by a single Hair
　　Turn Fate aside.　And once beneath the Car,
To us the Cash is neither Here nor There.

" Insure ! " they cry ; as though for You gone
　　hence,
Or Me, their cheque could furnish recompense !
　　Come, where yon great Policeman lifts his
　　Hand,
And cross the Road 'neath that Omnipotence !

From *This Funny World* by RAYMOND COULSON.

ON THE CARPET (OXFORD).

Don.

I HEAR, sir, and I fear the story true,
You have a cask of liquor in your room—
An act, you know, forbidden by the laws
And precepts of the University.

Student.

Alas ! in this I had no thought to err,
Or disobey your high authority ;
But needing strength—with all humility—
I sought advice of Æsculapius, who
Prescribed perennial draughts of double X.
This unknown quantity in double dose
I took *ad lib.*, and for convenience' kept
My physic near my bed.

Don.

           And have you found
The answer of expectancy and hope
In the renewal of virility ?

Student.

Aye, question not, nor have a doubt of that :
When first they placed the barrel in my room
I could not lift it, now with careless ease
I move it where I will !   A. H. M.

THE SUFFRAGETTE.

IF maidens sit in Parliament
    We shall be circumvented :
Who choose a Miss to represent
    Must be miss-represented.

How wisely nature, ordering all below,
Forbade the beard on woman's chin to grow,
For how could she be shaved, whate'er the skill,
Whose tongue would never let her chin be still ?

"Whenever I marry," said Suffragette Anne,
"I must really insist upon wedding *a man* ; "
But what if the men, and all men are but human,
Are equally nice about wedding *a woman* ?

THE BUILDING UP OF A MAN

MANY things go to **the Building up of a Man,** and as none of us have any choice in the selection of ancestors, we can only build upon the foundations laid for us by others. Chesterfield says "Style is the dress of thoughts," and Buffon that "The Style is the man." A well-known proverb declares that "what is bred in the bone will come out in the flesh"; and all these sayings go to show that outward appearances are largely the result of inward qualities, and that the highest attainment of human presentation is "the outward and visible sign of inward and spiritual grace." Shakespeare is responsible for the statement that "Some are born great, some achieve greatness, and some have greatness thrust upon them," and another writer has given us the phrase "The poet is born, not made." Shakespeare's divisions, however, suggest those of the fashionable world. Some are *born polite,* some *achieve politeness,* and some *have politeness thrust upon them.* Those " to the manner born " are the solid mahogany of human furniture; those who acquire politeness are the skin-deep fashionables of meaner woods, coated with mahogany veneer capable of equal polish, but less sound and enduring; those that have politeness thrust upon them are those whom accident or worse has raised above their proper sphere, and who, lacking quality, grain, and timbre of their own, are invested with all imaginable virtues by the fulsome flattery of fools.

Beginning at the beginning, then, and saying with Dr. Watts—himself a diminutive—in his *Horæ Lyricæ* :

> "Were I so tall to reach the pole,
>   Or grasp the ocean with my span,
> I must be measured by my soul :
>   The mind's the standard of the man,"

a very few words will suffice for that part of our subject, the treatment of which must be either unnecessary or futile. **Spirit and Temperament**

THE PROPORTIONS OF THE HUMAN FORM.

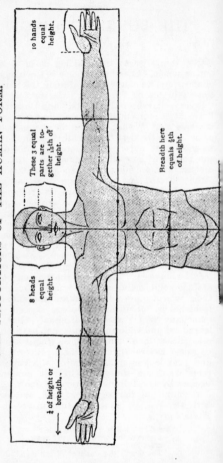

10 hands equal height.

These 3 equal parts are together ⅛th of height.

8 heads equal height.

Breadth here equals ¼th of height.

¼ of height or breadth.

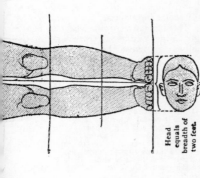

Head
equals
breadth of
two feet.

This diagram represents the exact proportions of the perfect human figure.

From PEARSON'S MAGAZINE.—*By Permission.*

have all to answer for here, and it is only needful to point out that **a healthy mind in a healthy body** is necessary to the expression of the higher feelings in the common courtesies of life. " Hope springs eternal in the human breast," says Pope, and the optimistic spirit is that which commends itself most readily to human companionship. Optimism shows itself in a hopeful attitude of mind, a bright aspect of countenance, and a cheerful manner of action. Pessimism is never long in writing care upon the face. If the world be, as it is often called, "a vale of tears," the mere obligations of courtesy and politeness impel us to bear our own burdens, and to do what we can to lighten those of others. " He who would have friends must show himself friendly," and the choice of friends, which is at the basis of social intercourse, is determined by affinities. The company of the cheerful is the most sought after, and most travellers on the world's highway recognise the wisdom of choosing companions of the happier sort.

> " Who goes my way, comrade true,
> Down the highway, 'neath the blue ?
> Mumbler, grumbler—you won't do !
> Fumbler, stumbler—not with you !
> Light of heart and nimble toed
> Foots it merrily down the road,
> Flat of foot and dull of head
> Trudges heavily home to bed.
> What oh ! Merriman ! Toe the line ;
> You're the very man ; foot it fine,
> Never fearful, rain or shine,
> Ever cheerful friend of mine."—A. H. M.

Next to a healthy mind A HEALTHY BODY is the desideratum, and here, as in the case of mental inheritance, our physical possibilities are limited by the bequeathment of our ancestors. An old scripture says, " Which of you by taking thought can add a cubit to his stature ? " and the impossible of old time remains impossible still. A cubit represents a foot or more in length, and were it possible for thought to add this measurement to the human body, the men of five feet in height amongst us would soon be the most thoughtful of all. And yet the body is capable of great development, and just so much as it is capable of it should surely receive. Graceful movement is as necessary to a perfect manner, as graceful thought and habitual grace

of carriage and action are to the united product
of a cultured mind and body.

It is not necessary nowadays to do more
than point out the advantages of **Physical
Culture**. Its general value in promoting health,
strength, and efficiency, is admitted upon
all hands, and its importance as a factor in
giving dignity of carriage and grace of movement will not be disputed. A short ode to
dumb bells given on page 144 may be referred
to in this connection. Exercise under due
restraint is the prime factor in the development
of most things, and qualified professional supervision is necessary to ensure wise restraint.
Athleticism has made many men, it has probably
marred more. Many an athlete is "all to pieces"
at forty years of age.

While this is true, one has only to compare the
average height of the young men and women of
to-day with those of fifty years ago, to see what
may be gained by the freer exercise of the limbs
in open-air sports. What the bicycle has done
for the legs, cricket and lawn tennis have done
for the arms; and the result of this and other
causes is an increase of the average height
of the men and women of the classes that
affect these recreations. That which raises the
standard of average offers a clear lead to those
who fall short of it, and if anno domini has not
already determined limitations "a word to the
wise is sufficient." All that the tailor may do is to
make the best he can of the figure he is called
upon to cover, and it is not by any means always
his fault when the results are unsatisfactory.

As a matter of interest we give on pp. 136-7
a diagram showing the true proportions of **The
Human Form Divine**, and having pictured the
outline we now propose to refer to some details
which are necessary to its healthy appearance.
Head foremost, we dive into the sea, and in
plunging into this subject, we will proceed head
first.

Heads and Faces—the Hair.—Few characteristics of the modern man mark him out more
distinctly from his forbears than his manner
of wearing his hair. Frequently he cannot keep
his hair on his head, and he will not keep it
upon his face. The former is to be regretted,
the latter is not without its advantages. Nothing

can ever make a bald head picturesque, and it seems a pity that the habit of shaving the chin does not appear to encourage the luxuriance of the growth on the head. The prophets who predict a hairless and toothless race do not open up to us a very inviting future. It is one of the advantages women have over men, that they are able so materially to vary their appearance by the different arrangement of their hair, and if men are to lose altogether their hirsuteness they will suffer a still greater disadvantage. One thing is certain, if we are in any real danger of losing the hair of the head, it becomes us to use every care we can for its preservation. In this, as in most, if not all other things, the advice of the specialist is the best guide. Preparations of various kinds are widely advertised, but they should only be used with professional approval. Careful washing and brushing are of course good for the hair. **The Shaven Face** certainly makes for cleanliness, but the question of shaving is necessarily one which must be left to individual taste. Every one is justified in grooming himself to the best advantage, and the hair upon the face may be made, like charity, to cover a multitude of sins." If the mouth is not all that its owner might wish, or if the teeth, though full in number—and health demands this—still leave something to be desired, a moustache may often be grown with advantage; and though it may be regarded merely as the lesser of two evils, it is still the lesser, and therefore the less disadvantageous. Scars, though sometimes marks of honour, are never "things of beauty," and beard and whiskers may well be grown for their obscuration. It is here that men have an advantage over women in the arrangement of the hair.

It should never be forgotten that the shape of the head and face are an indication of individuality, and hence it is wise in the growth and training of hair to preserve shape and form. The man with a pointed face is ill-advised to wear a broad flowing beard, and the man with a broad face will not as a rule advantage by following the example of the goat.

If it is decided to keep the face shaven, care must be taken to maintain the rule, for of all untidy things an untidy face is perhaps the worst.

When the hair is dark and of rapid growth it is especially necessary that the razor should be in frequent use. Those who find the use of the razor difficult or dangerous, should use a "safety," and the "Grilette," if its blades are changed with sufficient frequency, will be found readily equal to occasion.

In the preservation of health, as well as in the make-up of appearances, **The Teeth** play a very important part, and no one can afford to ignore them. The inconvenience, to say nothing of the pain, often incident to their proper care commonly leads to their neglect, but Nemesis nearly always follows. A fee paid to a competent dentist is always a good investment.

Eye Glasses, when required, should be worn for use, and not for ornament, and if the health of the eyes is to govern their employment, a pair is preferable to one. Affectation is always to be deprecated, and ostentation is always vulgar.

Face Massage is rather an idle amusement than a practical benefit. Anything that stimulates the natural functions is good within limits, and the muscles of the face may be benefited by occasional stimulus. All conditions of the face as a rule, whether they be wrinkles or pimples, require treatment from inside. The effects of face massage are hypnotic rather than aught else, and pass without permanent advantage.

The Body.—Passing from the head to the body, and attempting in the briefest possible manner to indicate the physiological causes of good carriage, the lungs and **the art of breathing** demand special attention. We are so much the creatures of habit, and pay so little intelligent attention to the observance of our natural functions, that notwithstanding lifelong practice very few adults know how to breathe, and yet the health and the appearance of the whole body depend upon full, healthy, and well-regulated respiration. To begin at the beginning, we have to return to the head, and note that the nose is the natural respiratory organ, and that when the face is in repose the mouth should always be closed. The stronger aboriginal races imposed the habit of breathing through the nose upon their children from their earliest years, and there can be no doubt that the gaping children of civilisation set traps for disease when they habitually keep the mouth open. The art of breathing cannot be dealt with here, but if a man is to have the full advantage of his physical endowment he must acquire the entire command of the whole of his lungs, and to do this he must practise breathing if not in the same way or to the same extent, certainly in the same direction as that pursued by the professional singer. The full use of the lungs gives the proper form to the upper part of the body, and this is an absolute essential of good carriage. If the client's habits induce a pigeon-breast no habits which the tailor can produce will make a good figure. **Diet and Exercise** are the two principal factors in promoting the healthy working of the human machine, and the healthy operation of all the functions is necessary to the building up of just so much of the perfect form as may lie within the range of individual possibility. Regularity and moderation make for health. Most men eat and drink more than is necessary to sustain healthy conditions, and few take sufficient exercise to maintain them. If the pigeon-breast is a thing to be avoided, the alderman's paunch should at least fail of encouragement. We condone the corporation because we have become callous to its ugliness, and are only reminded of it when we attend a Turkish bath, but we have only to recall the figure of the Apollo Belvedere, and to imagine the addition of a huge abdominal protuberance to see what a distortion a pot-belly is. Prevention is better than cure ; and for either, diet and exercise are the best medicine. Sport provides the pleasantest method of developing the principal muscles, and the many opportunities of physical culture already referred to may be trusted to do the rest. The hands will well repay care and attention, and **manicure** has much more to claim for itself than face-massage has. Except when gloved, the hands are almost always in sight, and a white hand well groomed is always a recommendation. Food, exercise, and sleep are the trinity of health, and each suffers by the loss of either one. The whole duty of man is to take himself as he finds himself, know himself, and understand himself, and then develop to the full extent of his possibilities all the powers he finds within himself in his own highest interest and for the service of his fellow-men.

Much has been written on the subject of **Clothes**, but the old truths remain. Good material looks better and wears longer than that which is inferior, and the practice of some who, with a view to change and variety, prefer two suits of a lesser quality to one of better substance at equal cost is not encouraging. Good make usually goes with good material, and real smartness requires both. The tailor does for the appearance what the doctor does for the health, and when employing either it is best to employ one in whom you have entire confidence, give him sufficient liberty and time to acquire a complete knowledge of your constitution, and then judge him by results. Neither health of body nor comeliness of appearance is to be secured by constantly changing treatment. But when ancestry has done all that it can, when a goodly figure has been well draped in the best of clothing, habit must make discipline easy if the best results are to be achieved.

It is the little things that show finish in all art and that add the charm of grace to costume. A good tailor working on a good model with good materials may be trusted to answer for the main building of a man's superstructure ; but it is hats, gloves, cuffs, collars, ties, and boots (see pp. 186–191) that put the finishing touches on a good appearance. Cheap silk hats are never a good investment, and good clean linen always repays cost and trouble. These, with good gloves that fit, and boots made to measure, will leave little else but manners to be added. **Slovenliness** must always be avoided. The man who is slovenly in dress or manner shows that he has not yet reached that degree of culture at which slovenliness becomes distasteful, and so proves that his past training has left something to be desired. Customs change, but laws remain. The fashions are one thing to-day, and another thing to-morrow, but smartness in the fashion of the time must always be the passport of the smart set. The beaux of all times have been those who have excelled in the smartness of neatness, if such a term may be allowed, and this is the reverse of the slovenliness of deshabille which so many young men affect.

SPORT.

> Not the laurel—but the race,
> Not the quarry—but the chase,
> Not the dice-cup—but the play
> May I heed, enjoy alway.
>
> Who misses or who wins the prize
>   Go lose or conquer as you can ;
> But if you fall or if you rise,
>   Be still, pray God, a gentleman.

DUMB-BELLS—amos r. wells.

> Dumb-bells, silent though ye be,
> Ring the chimes of health for me !
> Summon strength to muscles weak,
> Call the roses to my cheek ;
> Ring the languid bearing out,
> And ring in a body stout ;
> Where the hidden frailties lie,
> Sound alarm and bid them fly ;
> Feeble voice and shortened breath
> Toll their unlamented death ;
> Ring the happy marriage hour
> Wedding comeliness to power ;
> Sweeping free and wide and strong,
> Carol forth my matin song ;
> On your sides be written this :
> *Work is health* and *Health is bliss ;*
> Dumb-bells, silent though ye be,
> Ring the chimes of health for me !

THE BATSMAN'S ART—e. b. v. christian.

> Stand you erect, as doth befit a man ;
>   Firm let your right foot on the ground be set ;
>   Keep your left elbow up, nor e'er forget
> Keenly the bowler and the ball to scan,
> And hit not on a preconcerted plan.
>   Play a straight bat, so shall each ball be met
>   By the full blade.   Still at the practice net
> Play as you would if now the match began.
> Do not assault the Umpire.   Play to win,
>   Not to achieve a lordly average ;
> Pull not a fast, straight ball ; with care begin ;
> Answer at once your fellow-batsman's call ;
> Last, play not under, but above the ball.
>   So counsels you Polonius the sage.

DREAMS THAT I DREAM—E. B. V. CHRISTIAN.

WHEN in my dreams I take my stand
To guard the stumps in Fairyland,
I little fear the bowler's wile,
Nor dread the wicket-keeper's guile ;
They do not bowl me off my pad,
No catches from my glove are had ;
The hated " leg-before " is banned
In matches played in Fairyland.

I dream of many a glorious drive,
I feel the cut that goes for five ;
I hear the crowd's applauding roar
That follows oft a hit for four.
I practise the entrancing glide,
And win the battle for my side ;
We rarely fail to make a stand
When I go in—in Fairyland.

But when to bowl I take the ball,
How wondrous fast the wickets fall !
No liberties the batsmen take,
They do not disregard my break.
And though the pitch plays fast and true,
Leg-breaks come off, and balls cut through.
No batsmen *Wisden* knows could stand
The balls I bowl in Fairyland.

And though I bat the livelong day
To call of " Time," from call of " Play,"
They do not tire, nor envious grow,
Nor flag, nor feel the sport is slow ;
And though I bowl from first to last,
No shade of jealousy is cast ;
A joyous and contented band
Are we who play in Fairyland.

> In Fairyland ! In Fairyland !
>   On mortal turf I frankly own,
>   I never, never yet have shown
> A form one-twentieth as grand
> As I display in Fairyland !

By permission of Mr. J. W. Arrowsmith.

FOOTBALL—ALFRED H. MILES

It's Bumbletown and Dumbletown
  Are in the field to-day ;
And Dumbletown and Bumbletown
  Have come to see the play,
And Bumbletown has donned the blue,
  And Dumbletown the red,
And two-and-twenty stalwarts true
  Are to the battle sped.

And oh ! but 'twas a gallant sight
  As any eye could see :
The forces to the left and right,
  The colours waving free,
And first they cheered the bonny blue,
  And then the gaudy red,
And the green grass quivered as it grew,
  And the blue sky laughed o'erhead.

The forwards toe the limit line—
  Five giants in a row.
The backs and half-backs wait the sign—
  To hear the whistle blow.—
Before the keep at either end
  A son of Gath patrols,
All armour-clad in glove and pad,
  To save and keep the goals.

And now the whistle, then a cheer
  Across the welkin flung,
As Bumbletown and Dumbletown
  Let go with foot and tongue.
And then it's dribble as you can
  And pass as you are able ;
And " hold your own " and " mark your man,"
  And tackle, hustle, babel.

It's scuffle here and scuttle there,
  All up and down the field,
As Bumbletown and Dumbletown
  Alternate press and yield.
It's hurricane and earthquake too,
  As rival surges roll,
And fighting through, the red and blue
  Alternate score a goal.

For who shall turn the torrent down
  That dashes to the fore
When Neptune plays for Dumbletown
  And thunders up the shore ?

And who shall hope to win the crown
   And issue of the fray,
When Boreas plays for Bumbletown
   And keeps the waves at bay ?

For few can hold their heads erect,
   As swirls and tempest near,
When Dumbletown bears down direct,
   With Neptune in the rear.
And who can call his feet his own
   When, roaring in their track,
All Bumbletown comes sweeping down
   With Boreas at their back ?

See Bumbletown, another goal !
   And loud the clamours rise,
As Dumbletown insurgent roll,
   And score and equalise.
Another cheer for Bumbletown ;
   Fame's giddy height they climb,
For Dumbletown is " Tumbledown "
   Sharp on the call of time.

But who shall say that either lost
   On this eventful day ;
Though, battle-blown and tempest-tost.
   They both survive the fray !
And when at last the whistle blew,
   Out shone the setting sun,
And glory fell on red and blue,
For all were trusty, tried, and true ;
   So everybody won.

GOLF—T. B. SIMMINS (From *Golfer's Annual*).

LET football players risk their limbs,
   And roughly maul themselves about ;
Sportsmen have all their little whims,
   And some delight in rush and shout ;
But I prefer a quiet game,
   On velvet turf, by sounding sea ;
And what to me is wealth and fame
   When blithely driving from the tee !

Let cricketers the willow wield,
   Foiling the skilful bowler's art,
Whilst well-judged catch, or brilliant field,
   Raise thundering plaudits, each in part.

Yet, glorious cricket, though I love
 Thy manly game with all my heart,
Golf in my mind I place above :
 To thee I give the second part.

And when life's game comes to an end,
 And sports no more have charms for me,
May my poor spirit soar aloft,
 Like ball when driven from the tee,
And let my body lie below
 The bonny turf I oft have trod,
With a few words above, to show
 A golfer's bunkered 'neath the sod.

IN THE PLAYING-FIELDS—ALFRED H. MILES.

I

WE all start centre-forwards,
 And kick off very soon ;
And, wisely nursed, we win at first—
 And play the game till noon :
At " half-time "—*eheu fugaces*—
 Our forward play is o'er,
At " half," or " back," we wait attack,
 So to prevent a score.
Time finds us in the nets with lost control,
Death, centre-forward, kicks the final goal.

II

The last man in, and one to win,
 And the last over's last ball ;
O gentle bowler, send it in,
 A not too slow, or fast ball !
It came as fifty balls might come,
 A bowled-from-every-side ball !
I shut my eyes and drove it home,
 It skied, the long-field saw it dome,
 The umpire shouted, " Wide ball."
So in extremis, if my faith be tried,
When the last ball is bowled, Great Umpire,
  give it " wide."

THOROUGHBRED.

WE entered the world all naked and bare,
We go through the world with sorrow and care,
We go from the world and we know not where,
But if thoroughbred here we'll be thoroughbred
 there.

AFTER-DINNER STORIES

TELLING STORIES.

Good stories are always acceptable, and the art of story-telling is well worth cultivating. In recent years the practice of telling a few good stories instead of giving a recitation or making a speech has opened up a new field of opportunity for the raconteur. Some stories are good enough to tell themselves, that is to say, their humour is so broad and clear that it cannot fail of its mark, and the story only needs to be told simply and it will carry its own effect. Others again require some little art in delivery, that the main point may not be anticipated until the dramatic moment, when the incongruous surprise will provoke inevitable mirth. Three good stories are sufficient for one effort, for if more are wanted, an encore can easily be given. These may be arranged to include contrast, or to form sequence, and they may be all the better if a few appropriate words link them in natural connection.

Stories may be classified under various headings, and a certain unity is secured when all the stories told at one time are of one class. Irish stories, Scotch stories, sporting stories, dog stories, stories of lawyers, actors, artists, musicians, soldiers, sailors, and eccentrics. In the telling of stories the dog fancier runs the fisherman very close in the art of drawing the long bow. Whichever class of story is affected it is important to follow the positive, comparative, and superlative order of delivery. To anticipate the tit-bit is to produce an anti-climax, and the best should always be told last. The story-teller should always remember that "brevity is the soul of wit," and that all superfluous verbiage is so much discount on his success. In the following pages a few suggestive speech-stories are given.

Stories of Scotsmen.

I. Dr. Johnson has been credited with saying that the best view to be obtained in Scotland is that of the road to England, and English wit has often been exercised upon the supposed indisposition of the Scotsman who has come south to go " bok again."

II. That Scotsmen are well able to retort upon this charge was shown at a dinner of the Urban Club some years ago, when Hain Friswell, as chairman, twitted some young Scotsmen, including William Black and Robert Buchanan, who had recently arrived in London, with the national failing of not returning to their native heath. Robert Buchanan, in responding, remarked that the failing was not peculiar to Scotsmen, for he knew of a large number of Englishmen who visited Scotland on one occasion, and never came back again. "They went," he said, "to a place called Bannockburn."

III. A story which is supposed to illustrate the characteristics of the several nationalities is told of an Englishman, a Welshman, and a Scotsman who paid a visit to Ireland, and who upon their return brought with them mementoes of their trip. The Englishman brought a tobacco pouch with " God preserve old Ireland " on it ; the Welshman brought a mug with " A present from Dublin " on it ; but the Scotsman brought a knife and fork each with "London and North-Western Railway " on it.

IV. There is a good story of a certain Scot who, having fulfilled the years of an honourable career, passed away and was seen no more. Following precedent and natural instinct, he graduated to the wealthiest city within his ken, and begged the apostolic janitor to let him in. For some reason, I believe quite apart from his nationality, he was refused admission on the technical ground that his name was not on the register, or that, all Scotsmen being more or less of the same name, he could not be identified.

Not having much choice, he descended the hill, and approached the only other city he knew of in the neighbourhood, but only to receive the same answer and for the same alleged reasons. Weary and disconsolate, it is said he sat down on the doorstep, and began to cry. "Boo-oo-oo-oo," brought a crowd of little devils round him in a moment, all of whom attempted to cheer him up with the assurance that he never need pretend to be good any more, and that he would never again have to suffer from the cold. On ascertaining that he had been denied even these advantages, they still expressed their surprise that he should weep at being excluded from the nether world. Whereupon he began to cry again and said: "But, boo-oo-oo-oo, what am I to do? I don't want to have to go back to Scotland."

IRISHISMS.

I. "So you're an early riser, Pat?" "I am that, yer 'onner, and me father was an early roiser before me." "Oh! your father was an early riser before you, was he, Pat?" "Ah! he was that, yer 'onner. Why, if he'd gone to bed a little later he'd 'a' met himself gettin' up in the mornin', 'e would." "And how is your father, Pat?" "Me father, sor, he's dead this long toime, he is." "Dead, is he, Pat? and how long ago might that be?" "Faith, yer 'onner, if he'd lived till next Thursday week he'd 'a' been dead two years and a half, he would." "And what are you working at now, Pat?" "I'm workin' on the railway, yer onner!" "On the railway, are you, Pat? Well, that will be a good job done." "It will that, yer 'onner! When the new loin's opened you'll be able to get to London and back quicker than you can stay at home, you will."

II. "What's yours?" said the foreman as the boys knocked off work for the night. "Mine's a pint," says Tom; "And mine's a pint, too," says Dick. "And what's yours, Pat?" "Och! I'll just have a mouthful, yer 'onner!" said the Irishman. "No, you won't," said the foreman (he knew Pat's mouth), "you'll have just the same as the others." On turning out of doors Pat's movements were observed to be somewhat circuitous, and the foreman said to him, "Pat, I'm afraid you'll find that road longer than you expect." "Longer, yer 'onner? It's not that that's troublin' me; it's the width that's destroyin' me entoirely!"

III. From drinking to fighting is not a very far cry at any time, and Pat had not proceeded far before he had a difference with a nigger and went out into the road to settle it. According to the articles of war it was arranged that either combatant could end the fight by calling out "sufficient," and, with this proviso, they went at it "hammer-and-tongs." It was a very equal match, and the issue was long doubtful, but at last the nigger shouted "sufficient," upon which Pat exclaimed, with intense disgust, "Begorrah! and I've been troin' to think of that word for a quarter of an hour!"

STORIES OF LAWYERS.

I. A lawyer retired from his profession the other day and, having made his money out of ruined estates, bought one and set about repairing the ruins. Not wishing to maintain the identity of the place, he sought a title for his mixture of old stone and new stucco. Some one suggested "Dunrobbin Castle." He thought about it, but decided not to adopt it. He did not wish to convey the idea that he was not still open to business if it was sufficiently promising.

II. Another lawyer—or was it the same—having won a case involving a hundred pounds, deducted eighty pounds as his charges, and, handing the remaining twenty to his client, said : "I am your friend, sir. I cannot charge you my full fee; I knew your father." The client took the balance with no very good grace, but he recognised that things might have been worse, for he said as he took it : "Thank goodness you didn't know my grandfather."

III. One day, at the table of the late Dr. Pease, just as the cloth was being removed, the subject of conversation happened to turn on mortality amongst lawyers. "We have lost," said a gentleman, "not less than six eminent barristers in as many months." Whereupon the Dean, who was very deaf, and had not heard the remark, rose immediately and pronounced the grace—"For this and every other mercy, the Lord's name be praised!"

IV. If we could be quite sure that we should be immune from legal worries in the next world we might feel encouraged to endure what we have to suffer here, but apparently we have no guarantee of freedom from interference even there. It is said that some time ago the amenities of heaven were much disturbed by the frequent incursion of little devils, who climbed over the walls when no one was looking, and, scooting down among the angels, caused all kinds of scandal and annoyance. Complaints were made to the apostolic janitor, who protested that he was quite unable to cope with the difficulty, whereupon he was instructed to apply for an injunction. Still the annoyance went on without abatement. Still the little devils continued to climb over the walls when no one was looking and scooting down among the angels played all manner of pranks with harps and haloes and all other movable properties. Again the janitor was told that such things must not be. Indeed he was told that the character of the place was suffering, and that it was not nearly so select as it was before he held the keys. Retorting, with some warmth, he was asked why he had not applied for an injunction. "I have, I have!" was his passionate reply, "but it's no use. There are too many lawyers on the other side."

BEFORE THE CORONER.

I. A coroner was holding an inquest on the body of a man who had destroyed his life by hanging, and, after hearing the evidence of the police, always taken first, he called the man who had called the police, and interrogated him : "Tell us what occurred," said the great functionary, leaning back in his chair with a look of benign encouragement on his face. "Well, sir," he said, "it was like this: I was goin' down to the Red Lion for my mornin' pick-me-up when I see the defendant hangin' to a barn door!" "Yes," said the coroner, "and what did you do?" "Me, sir? I went and fetched a policeman!" "You went and fetched a policeman," exclaimed the coroner. "Why on earth didn't you cut him down?"

" Cut him down, your 'onner ? " said the astonished witness, " Why, he wasn't dead then ! "

II. A young man, who had true humanitarian feelings, was much concerned on account of his brother's tendency to suicide. Constantly on the alert, he was one night disturbed by hearing unusual sounds from his brother's bedroom, which was situated immediately above his own. Jumping out of bed, he ran upstairs and entered his brother's room, when he found, to his horror, a rope suspended to a big nail in the wall, and encircling his brother's waist. " What are you doing ? What are you doing ? " cried the interrupter in an agony of dismay. " Oh ! " said his brother, with tears in his voice, " it's no use ; I can't stand it any longer. I'm going to make away with myself, and the sooner the better." " Well, but," said the interrupter, " you must be mad. You shouldn't put the rope round your waist, but your neck." " My neck," cried the astonished penitent ; " not me ! I tried it there, and it nearly choked me ! "

TACT.

We are all called upon at times to deliver ill-news, and the supreme tact of the wisest sympathy is often subject to severe strain. Many illustrations might be given of attempts to extenuate circumstance and postpone shock, but it is doubtful if a better could be cited than the following story, which has run the round of the clubs of late. It proves at least that there are ways of putting things which may be trusted to prepare the mind by easy stages for the final blow, which may fall the lighter for the graduated process.

A gentleman who had been spending some months abroad, without receiving communications from home, arrived one evening at a country railway station, where he was met by his groom with a stylish dogcart, to enable him to complete his journey. " Glad to see yer back, sir," said the groom, and his master expressed his satisfaction at coming home once more. " You've been away a long time, sir," said the groom feelingly. " Well, yes, Jim, three months ; but three months is not very long after all." " It's a long time in the country where nothing ever happens, sir." "Ah well, I suppose it is, Jim; but what's the news now I have come back?" "Well, I don't know as there's any particular news, sir, but poor old Carlo's dead!" "Carlo's dead, is he? He was a good dog in his time, was old Carlo, but he was thirteen years old, Jim, and you can't expect a dog to live much longer than that." "Well, no, sir, I s'pose not, but it was the way he died that upset me." "The way he died? Why, how was that, Jim?" "He were burnt to death, sir!" "Burnt to death, Jim? Why, however did that happen?" "Well, sir, it were the mornin' after the old barn were burnt down, as we were rakin' over the ashes we found his poor old body burned to a cinder." "What! is the old barn burned down, Jim?" "Aye, that it is, sir, and a fine flare it was, too!" "But whatever set fire to the barn, Jim?" "Well, I don't know, sir, but they do say as it was the flames from the 'All what set fire to the barn!" "The flames from the Hall, Jim. Is the Hall burnt down, too?" "Aye, that it is, sir, and I never see such a conflagration!" "Well, but how did the Hall catch fire?" "Well, I don't know, sir, but they do say it was the wind a-blowin' the curtains agin the candles what was round the corfin what set fire to the 'All!" "Whose coffin, Jim?" "Oh, it were your mother's corfin, sir!" "My mother's coffin; and is my mother dead then?" "Aye, that she is, sir, and she didn't want no cremation neither!" "But what was the matter with her, Jim? She was well enough when I went away." "A trifle weak at the 'eart, sir, if you remember, and when she heard as your misses had joined the suffragettes, she reg'lar collapsed, she did, and that's all about it. But 'ere we are, sir, at last, and I'm very glad to see yer back at the old 'ome once again."

MISSIONARY.

I. A fervid orator appealing for more workers in the mission field invited any who were desirous of devoting themselves to the work to remain after the conclusion of the meeting. As the congregation dispersed an earnest, intelligent-looking lad made his way nervously towards the platform, and the orator, without waiting for a word of explanation, began congratulating the lad upon his noble resolve to devote his life to the cause of the heathen. A moment's pause gave the boy a chance, when he stammered : "Please, sir, it isn't that ; but do you happen to have any foreign stamps ? "

II. A little girl was once collecting for foreign missions, but was forbidden by her mother to ask people for money. She might tell people she was collecting, and then if they gave her money she might take it for the object she had in view. One day she called upon a friend of the family, who was a man of means, and who was aware of her mother's restriction, and, intending to give the child a subscription, he put a five-pound note, a sovereign, a half-sovereign, and a five-shilling piece on the table, and asked her which of these she thought he ought to give her. The little girl said she did not know which he *ought* to give her, but, pointing to the sovereign, she added, "I should like to have that one, but I shouldn't like to lose it, so (pointing at the bank-note) if you don't mind wrapping it up in that piece of paper I'm sure it will be quite safe."

MATRIMONIAL.

I. The young man was quite eligible, and the fond father quite anxious to improve the occasion. "You know," said the old man, "I mean to do my duty by my girls. They won't go empty-handed when they leave my door. There's Annie, for instance—nice girl, Annie, she's thirty years old. Annie shall have a thousand pounds when she's married. Then there's Mary ; she's thirty-five. I've always meant to give Mary two thousand, and I won't go back on my word ; and as for Jane, well, she's forty, and ought to have been married long ago. I won't stop short of five thousand to see her comfortably settled." The young man, who had betrayed a growing interest in the narrative, paused a moment, and then, leaning forward, said in quiet confidence, "You don't happen to have one about sixty, do you ? "

II. Jones received a telegram from his wife, "Mother is at the gates of death. Reply paid." Jones replied, "Pull her through ! "

TOASTS.

NATIONAL AND PATRIOTIC.

THE UNITED KINGDOM.

MAY the Rose of England fairer blow,
And Scotland's thistle taller grow;
May Erin's shamrock brighter shine,
And Cambria's leek with all entwine,
To form a votive wreath to lie
On Freedom's breast, where all would die.—*M.*

IRELAND.

Here's all that I wish thee,
   Great, glorious and free,
First flower of the earth,
   And first gem of the sea.—*Moore.*

Here's to the land of the shamrock so green;
Here's to each lad and his darling colleen;
Here's to the ones we love dearest and most,
And may God save old Ireland! an Irishman's
   toast.

SCOTLAND.

To "Scotia!" my dear, my native soil!
For whom my warmest wish to heaven is sent,
Long may thy hardy sons of rustic toil
Be blest with health and peace and sweet
   content.—*Burns.*

We toast ye, the nicht, the hill and the heather,
The land o' the bonnet, the plaid and the
   feather,
The land o' the mountain, the stream, and the
   river,
The land of our ancestors, Scotland for ever!
              G. W. McLaren.

WALES.

Here's to the Principality of Wales,
Her native wealth, her lovely hills and dales,
Her gift of song, her harp of honoured name,
Her olden industries, her ancient fame.—*M.*

IMPERIAL FEDERATION.

Now we pledge the hundred Englands
    Up and down the sea,
And the spirit that can bring lands—
    Federated—Free—
Into one Imperial Union
    For the good of all,
Strong in brotherly communion
    Let what will befall.—*M.*

AUSTRALIA.

We all are English, though new Melbourne poses
    Upon Port Phillip as a southern queen,
And old, in dells of Derbyshire still dozes
    A fit handmaiden for a rustic scene.
We all are English, born in one great union
    Of blood and language, history and song,
All English, and to cherish our communion
    We should present a common front to wrong.
                                    Douglas Sladen.

CANADA.

Here's to the land of the rock and the pine;
    Here's to the land of the raft and the river;
Here's to the land where the sunbeams shine,
    And the night is bright with the north light's
        quiver.
Here's to the buckwheat that smokes on her
        board;
    Here's to the maple that sweetens her story;
Here's to the scythe that she swings like a
        sword,
    And here's to the fields where she gathers
        her glory.—*W. Wye Smith.*

ENGLAND AND AMERICA.

May Peace for evermore abide,
    And nothing but the sea divide.—*M.*

ENGLAND AND FRANCE.

Our ancient foe, our modern friend,
    So may she bide until the end.—*M.*

ENGLAND AND GERMANY.

Two sturdy comrades scorning jealous fears,
So may we weather all succeeding years.—*M.*

FREEDOM.

To Freedom—everywhere it holds its own,
    By cot or castle, ingleside or throne.—*M.*

TOASTS SOCIAL AND DOMESTIC.

Here's to the debt we can never pay—For the care of childhood, the counsel of youth, and the love of a lifetime.

Duty's toast—above all others,
All upstanding, boys—Your Mothers.—*M.*

Here's to the Home—A man's kingdom, a child's paradise, and a woman's world.

Where love builds a nest there is ever a home,
And the head on the breast has no longing to
    roam.—*M.*

May we all draw prizes in the lottery of marriage, and find in true companionship the secret of happy life.

Here's to the girl with the heart and smile
Who makes this bubble of life worth while.

Here's to Love—the only fire against which there is no insurance.

Here's to Love—a thing divine,
    Description makes it but the less;
'Tis what we feel but can't define,
    'Tis what we know but can't express.

May the sunshine of plenty dispel the clouds of care, and the hand of prudence steer clear of the rocks of disaster.

As we sail on the sea of emotion,
    Whenever, wherever we roam,
May our joys be as deep as the ocean,
    Our sorrows as light as its foam.—*M.*

Here's to this little world of ours, which is not growing worse to the men and women who are doing their best to make it better.

It's not so bad a world as some would make it,
And, whether good or ill, is how we take it.—*M.*

May we draw upon content for the deficiencies of Fortune, and learn to be frugal without the teachings of necessity.

Then fortune will serve to a tittle,
    Though wealth may be never increased,
Contentment will find in a little,
    Enough is as good as a feast.—*M.*

Here's to Riches without pride, and Poverty without meanness.

An accident, a lucky star
    May lead us to the Abbey's niches,
Not what we *have*, but what we *are*,
    Is the imperishable riches.—*Pomeroy.*

May we look forward to better things without disparaging the things that are, and may the thorns of life only give us a greater love for its flowers.

Here's to the heart that beats the same
Whether it win or lose the game.—*M.*

Here's to a strong Fleet for Home Defence ; Companionship in harbour, Comradeship on the high seas, and Friendship at every port.

When friendship, love, and truth abound
    Among a band of brothers,
The cup of joy goes gaily round,
    Each shares the bliss of others. . . .
On halcyon wings our moments pass,
    Life's cruel cares beguiling,
And Time lays down his scythe and glass,
    In glad good humour smiling.
How grand in age, how fair in youth,
Are holy Friendship, Love, and Truth.
                                Montgomery.

May we cherish friendship with a jealous care, and ever keep strict guard over the avenues of suspicion.

Here's health to all those that I love,
And health to all those that love me.
Here's health to all those that love those that
    I love
And all those that love those that love me.

Here's to the memories of the past, the joys of the present, and the hopes of time to come.

A health to the future, a sigh for the past,
We love to remember, we hope to the last,
And for all the bare lies that the almanacs hold,
While we've youth in the heart, we can never
    grow old.   *G. W. Holmes.*

INDOOR AMUSEMENTS

INDOOR GAMES FOR ADULTS.

To all active temperaments, something to do is a necessity, and to compel such to inactiivty is to inflict them with boredom. But here, as in everything else, " variety is the charm of life," and the minor social functions such as " At-Homes " and unpretentious evening parties are in danger of becoming wearisome inflictions if new interests are not constantly introduced. Such games as Table Tennis, and games of this class require more physical skill and energy than many people care to employ on indoor recreations, and so become the exclusive enjoyment of the younger and more vigorous. Competitions in mental skill afford quieter means of occupation, which appeal with greater acceptance to the older members of the company, and as in the nature of things, many of these can be played without in any way interfering with the amusements more congenial to others, they may often be employed together, and so cover the whole ground of recreative necessity. To facilitate such amusements, the publishers of fancy stationery have issued materials for **card competition games** in considerable variety and requiring varying degrees of skill, specimens of which by their courtesy are included in the following pages. To those who find sufficient pleasure in the exercise, prizes may be no inducement, but as a rule in these days they excite competition and add to interest. In all cases they should be of moderate value and be more treasured as souvenirs of happy occasions than for their intrinsic value. The following cards, published by Messrs. Delgardo & Co., Ltd., are supplied in boxes of twelve with pencils and cards attached, and with a card containing a key to the solution of the several puzzles. In the following examples the answers are given in the right-hand columns in the space left blank on the actual cards.

Muddled Maxims.

EXPLANATION.—*Each group of letters represents a well-known proverb ; the words of which are in their proper order but the letters of each word are transposed*

EETRBTELATTANHREEVN	.	Better late than never
VEEYRODGAHSHSIDYA .	.	Every dog has his day
LITLSTREWASRUNEPED	.	Still waters run deep

This Game consists of 21 Proverbs

Tangled Towns.

Letters spell name of town when properly arranged		County in which the town is situated		Name of Town
THYOAMRU	.	Norfolk	. .	YARMOUTH
TNOSDHEU	.	Essex	. .	SOUTHEND
SOCNETRAD	.	Yorkshire	.	DONCASTER

This Game consists of 24 Towns

Tangled Titles.

Letters which spell title of book when properly arranged		Name of Author		Title of Book
LEEWRVYA	.	*Walter Scott .*	.	Waverley
LKEUOBEHAS	.	*Charles Dickens*	.	Bleak House
LEHMAP	.	*Lord Lytton*	.	Pelham

This Game consists of 24 Titles

A Musical Romance.

In this game the musical terms here printed in capitals are left blank spaces

The young people at the sea-town of BARmouth had watched with interest the attentions paid by Mr. BEN MARCATO to Miss ANDANTE, so that when the engagement was announced her friends did not REST until they had sent NOTES of congratulation. (*Numerous words to fill in.*)

A Newspaper Romance.

In this game the names of the newspapers or periodicals here printed in capitals are left blank spaces

The young people of QUEENstown were much interested in the movements of an eligible young bachelor, who was reputed rich and anxious to get married, so that when at last they heard he had met THE LADY of his choice, all THE WORLD & HIS WIFE flocked to congratulate them both. (*Numerous words to fill in.*)

A " Novel " Letter.

In this game the names of the books here printed in capitals are left blank spaces

DEAR JESS (*Rider Haggard*)

Only last week my sister and I, and OUR MUTUAL FRIEND (*Dickens*) decided to go for A TRAMP ABROAD (*Mark Twain*), so here we are, in THE HEART OF ROME (*M. Crawford*) and simply delighted with all we have seen. (*Forty words to fill in.*)

Buried Christian Names (Women).

A well-known Christian name of a woman lies hidden in each sentence. Find the Name.

It was a ripping race . . .	GRACE
No pastry can beat rice pudding .	BEATRICE
She had a nice berth and voyage .	BERTHA

This Game consists of 29 Questions

Buried Christian Names (Men).

A well-known Christian name of a man lies hidden in each sentence. Find the Name.

The bird lined her nest with moss .	ERNEST
On the step, hens were sitting .	STEPHEN
Her bertha was made of fine lace .	HERBERT

This Game consists of 28 Questions

Think it Out—Heliotrope.

The answers consist of words formed from the letters in HELIO-TROPE

Looked for north and south . .	POLE
To marry romantically . .	ELOPE
What keeps us from despair . .	HOPE

This Game consists of 22 Questions

Honeysuckle Petals.

The answers consist of words spelt with letters found in the word HONEYSUCKLE

Much heard during an Election. .	HECKLE
Punishment by an angry mob .	LYNCH
A favourite sport . . .	HOCKEY

This Game consists of 40 Questions

Aggravating Rates.

Each answer must be a word ending with RATE

A rate that gets worse . .	DEGENERATE
A rate that dwindles to nothing .	EVAPORATE
A rate that is not excessive .	TEMPERATE

This Game consists of 40 Questions

The Kingly Game.

Each answer must be a word ending with KING

A king who was long besieged .	MAFEKING
A king who torments others .	PROVOKING
A merry, uproarious king .	ROLLICKING

This Game consists of 40 Questions

The Game of the Perplexing Ass.

Each answer must be a word beginning with ASS (or AS pronounced as ASS)

A ready, helping ass . .	ASSISTANT
An ass used by the Kaffirs .	ASSEGAI
An ass cut in halves . .	ASUNDER

This Game consists of 30 Questions

Troublesome Imps.

Each answer must be a word beginning with I M P

An imp that cannot be taken	IMPREGNABLE
An imp that does things off-hand	IMPROMPTU
An imp that is easily touched	IMPRESSIONABLE

This Game consists of 34 Questions

The Game of Pros and Cons.

The answer in each case must be a word commencing with either Pro or Con

A Scottish Official	PROVOST
A Piece of Music	CONCERTO
A Geographical Term	PROMONTORY

This Game consists of 24 Questions

A Great Society Bazaar.

Each answer must be the name of a Periodical

What was the Bazaar called	VANITY FAIR
What was sold at the refreshment stall ?	TIT-BITS
Which paper gave the most realistic account ?	THE GRAPHIC

This Game consists of 26 Questions

A Menu for all Sorts and Conditions of People.

Each answer must be a food suitable for the different class of people mentioned

The food for poachers	POACHED EGGS
What birds do undergraduates like	LARKS
The shell-fish liked by all athletes	MUSSELS

This Game consists of 26 Questions

See-Saw.

Each " SAW " is a well-known proverb which will rhyme with the " SEE "

SEE	SAW
Trial brings a blessing down	No cross, no crown
To find the needy do not roam	Charity begins at home
Squire stampeded, scullion ran	Like master, like man

This Game consists of 20 Proverbs

A Great Universal Supply Store.

The answer is in each case the title of a well-known novel

What was the store called (Dickens)	Old Curiosity Shop
Where was it situated (R. Whiteing)	No. 5 John Street
When was it opened (Charles Kingsley)	Two Years Ago
Who provided the capital (W. Besant)	Ready Money Mortiboy

This Game consists of 24 Questions

Messrs. Delgardo publish over fifty varieties of card games, and are continually adding to their list. These can be procured through any fancy stationer.

Other varieties of parlour games are issued from other houses. The following are from the list of Messrs. Goodall & Sons, and may be had of all fancy stationers

The "Paper" Game.

Each question must be answered by the title of a well-known Paper

The highest in the land	The King
The leaders of fashion	The Smart Set
The dread of all nations . . .	The War Cry
A burden on the rates . . .	The Idler

This Game consists of 41 Questions

A Stage Ball.

The answer to each question is a well-known Play

Where was the ball given ? . .	Haddon Hall
Who sent the invitations ? . .	The Private Secretary
What did every mother hope to secure for her daughter ? .	The Catch of the Season
Who served the refreshments ?	The Geisha

This Game consists of 40 Questions

Shamrock.

Each answer is composed of letters in the word SHAMROCK.

A faithful serving man and true,	
'Twas feared he liked the widows too .	Sam (Weller)
Something of early Gothic style	
And oft describes a maiden's smile .	Arch
Wild waves dash o'er me—spray so light	
Or placed upon the mountain height .	Rock

This Game consists of 24 Questions

English Cathedrals.

The answer to each question is a well-known English Cathedral

Destroyed by fire—restored by Wren	
I rise above the haunts of men .	St. Paul's
The Apostle's town . . .	Peterborough
Irish mourning and a meadow .	Wakefield

This Game consists of 29 Questions

"On the Cards."

Each answer to be a term used at Cards, especially at Bridge

What did simple Mary lose ? . .	Heart
What did she play for ? . .	Love
As her cards were so bad what did she say ? .	"I leave it"

This Game consists of 24 Questions

Celebrity Puzzles.

Couplets descriptive of the Celebrity or a Play on the Name

His name is recalled by an ancient town,	
His works are of great and lasting renown .	Carlyle
Give a weapon sharp a quiv'ring motion,	
My name is known from ocean unto ocean .	Shakespeare
A domestic article gives the sign	
Of a nation's hero—yours and mine .	Kitchener

This Game consists of 24 Questions

An Anglais-Français Story.

Under this heading Messrs. Goodall & Sons publish a double card upon which is printed an account of the festivities held in honour of the coming of age of a young Frenchman. The story is told in English, and blanks are left for the insertion of French words to complete the sense. These are all words in common use by English-speaking people, but as seventy words are required to complete the story, and the prize (if any) must go to the competitor who fills in the largest number in a given time, it will be seen that the competition is a real one, and one likely to create great interest. Some sentences run as follows, "The company included all the (*élite*) of the neighbourhood." "The (*costumier*) had turned out the most (*chic*) gowns, absolutely (*à la mode*), etc., etc., etc.

Other Card Games are provided by the same firm which, however, it is impossible to describe in detail here. **All About Ma**, 32 questions; **The Game of Cities**, 20 questions; **A Musical Tea**, 33 questions; **A Party at the Zoo**, 24 questions; **A Periodical Letter**, 64 questions; **An English Garden**, 28 questions; **Current Jokes**, 22 questions; **An Alphabetical Romance**, 26 questions; **Reverse**, 30 questions; **A Novel Fleet**, 24 questions, etc., etc., etc. These cards, with pencil and tassel complete, are sold in boxes containing twelve cards and a key card, by all fancy stationers.

Acting Charades are performed in several ways. In one form a scene is devoted to each syllable, and a final scene to the whole word, and the syllables and the word are not only acted but uttered at least once in the scenes by which they are represented; in another form the syllables and the final word are acted but not spoken; and in a third the syllables are sounded in the several scenes, but the whole word is not uttered in the final. Either plan may be adopted with a view to simplifying or obscuring the issues, as words may vary in difficulty of treatment. Whichever plan is adopted the course intended to be pursued should be made quite clear to the audience, who should be told the number of syllables and scenes which will represent the word chosen. The best acting charades are those which can be so arranged that the several scenes are consecutive incidents in one story, and so form a short play. Let us suppose that the word "wedlock" is selected for the purpose. The first scene may well be a reception after a wedding, at which the father of the bride may say to the happy pair casually, "Well, you're wed at last, and I hope you will be very happy," shortly after which the scene may end. The second scene may disclose the bride (a month later) seated at her husband's desk, in which she finds, among his letters, a lock of hair. At this point one of her late bridesmaids enters and fans her jealousy to flame, advising her to demand immediate explanation, and insist on knowing at once whose lock of hair it is, after which she leaves. The third scene is the husband's return, and the first quarrel, during which the benedict, quite unconscious of the *casus belli*, may say, "Well! if this is wedlock, I think I had better have kept out of it," after which the wife produces the lock of hair, which the husband immediately recognises as a curl cut from a pet dog he once possessed, and satisfactory explanation follows. This is a rather obvious rendering, and few will fail to solve the riddle, but it illustrates the advantage of making the scenes form a consecutive narrative, in fact, a novelette of real life. Of course this is not always possible, and three or more separate scenes having no connection at least give opportunity for contrast and ordered variety.

Words for Acting.—Sky-lark, snap-shot, mad-cap, pad-lock, bond-age, ear-ring, neck-lace, night-mare, black-mail, war-lock, man-hood, child-hood, grand-child, grand-mother, book-worm, book-maker, van-guard, war-spite, home-sick, pot-luck, kind-red, wel-come, wel-fare, fare-well, court-ship, heart's-ease, sweet-hearts, love-knot, check-mate, moon-struck, ill-will, sea-son, orphan-age, highway-man, pen-man-ship, ring-leader, work-man-ship, thorough-bred, cast-away, co-nun-drum, Shake-speare, Shy-lock, Fal-staff, Touch-stone, Ham-let ; also words beginning with in, doubling the n— in-tent, in-mate, in-dul-gent, in-constant ; words ending in man, as bond-man, bell-man, foot-man, fire-man, states-man, watch-man, prize-man, sports-man; words ending in smith, as gold-smith, gun-smith, silver-smith, black-smith; names of places, as Ox-ford, Cam-bridge, High-gate, Lady-well, Smith-field, Folk-stone, Swan-age, Black-pool, Red-hill, Hunting-don, Scar-borough, and some proper names—as Good-child, Well-beloved, Young-husband, Thorough-good, etc., etc., etc.

Acting Proverbs are played by one or more performers. In their simple form each proverb is acted by a single player, separately, but in some cases a proverb may require more than one performer for its representation. As a rule, the proverbs are performed in dumb-show, but sometimes they are accompanied with monologue. As an example of a proverb acted by one person in dumb-show, take the following rendering of "Honesty is the best policy." A servant girl begins dusting a drawing-room with a feather broom, when she discovers her master's purse on the mantel-piece. She opens it and counts the money, hesitates, puts it back again, and goes on with her work. She again opens the purse and takes out a sovereign, hesitates once more, puts it back again, and flies temptation by rushing out of the room.

The following **proverbs suitable for dumb-show** performance by single players will suggest their own treatment. "A bad workman always quarrels with his tools" (player imitates the use of saw, plane, chisel, hammer, throwing them impatiently aside, one after the other; finally cuts or hammers his fingers, and dances about with rage). "All is not gold that glitters" (a chemist pretends to test with acid various articles borrowed from the audience, and returns some with a nod of approval, and some with a shake of the head). "What can't be cured must be endured" (a tramp with a crutch, a loose sleeve hanging, and a patch over his eye). "Forewarned is fore-armed" (preparing for burglars). "A penny saved is a penny gained" (transfer a letter from a box marked "post" to one marked "delivery"). "The pitcher that goes oft to the well is broken at last" (imitate the drawing of water at a well, and the dropping of the pitcher on return—lady's proverb). **Proverbs accompanied by monologues.**—"A contented mind is a continual feast" (an old-age pensioner). "Fools and their money are soon parted" (a ruined spendthrift). "When the wine is in, the wit's out" (silly intoxication). "A miss is as good as a mile" (a disappointed marksman). "A guilty conscience needs no accuser" (a criminal determining to give himself up to justice). "Where there's a will, there's a way" (optimism under difficulties, and determination to get on). **Proverbs for several characters** may be prepared with all the elaboration of charades or private theatricals, and almost any proverb may be attempted. "Handsome is as handsome does," "One good turn deserves another," "A friend in need is a friend indeed," "Anything for a quiet life" may suggest their own treatment.

Acting Rhymes are played singly, as proverbs are, but where the rhyme requires it, the rhymer may be allowed to invite the help of another player from the audience. The action is dumb-show. As rhyming words capable of being acted are not always numerous, six or eight players will often be sufficient for one round. One of the company names a word or a syllable, and each player in turn acts a rhyme to it. Care must be taken in the selection of words and sounds, as some admit of too few rhymes to be practical. The sound AKE suggests wake, quake, shake, rake, break, take, bake, and snake, all of which may be acted. Other sounds and rhymes are ANCE—dance, glance, prance, lance, trance, advance, intemperance; OWE—bow, mow, throw, row, blow, hoe, roe, stow, sew; ITE—bite, fight, flight, fright, write, recite, delight. E—bee, flee, knee, free, see, sea, tee, tea, plea, glee. AD—bad, mad, glad, sad, dad, fad, pad. ACE—face, grimace, race, chase, interlace, trace, embrace. AIN—pain, stain, cane, plane, vain, chain, sprain, skein. SAGE, age, rage, wage, gage, cage, stage, page. IDE—hide, ride, stride, bride, guide, bestride, divide. END—bend, rend, blend, mend, defend, descend, distend.—ENCE—fence, defence, indolence, eloquence, consebuence, benevolence.

Games New and Old.—New games are all more or less modifications of old games, just as new tricks are usually adaptations of old puzzles. These new-old games, too, have a way of reverting to their original forms, and there are not a few who affirm that the old games are the best. This must be our excuse if the reader, looking for the impossible, something new under the sun, finds much in the following pages with which he is familiar.

Viva-voce Games are often of more active interest than card games; they are more noisy, and therefore, as some would say, less dull. **Man and His Object** is one of these. Two persons, preferentially a lady and a gentleman, go out of the room, and the company present decide upon some man or woman and some object characteristic of and belonging to the man or woman chosen, which shall form the basis of the puzzle. These subjects may be historical, political, literary, scientific, or general. They may be universal or local. A great deal of amusement may often result from the choice of some well-known member of the company present, provided, of course, the person chosen does not object. Very funny results have often followed the choice of one of the persons appointed to guess the puzzle. The man or woman may be a well-known character in fiction, but the object should always be tangible.

The following list of men and objects may be suggestive. Alfred the Great and the burnt cakes, King John and Magna Charta, Christopher Columbus and America, George Washington and his hatchet, James Watt and the steam engine, George Stephenson and the locomotive, William Tell and his apple, Dick Whittington and his cat, Wellington and his boots, Nelson and his telescope, Maxim and his gun, Dumont and his airship, Sir John Franklin and the North-West Passage, Peary and the North Pole, Mr. Gladstone and his collars, Mr. Chamberlain and his eye-glass, etc., etc., etc.

Local subjects may include the rector or vicar of the parish and some object connected with his church, or the mayor of the borough and something appertaining to the Town Hall. A local artist and his pictures, a local musician and his violin or piano, a local miser and his money.

The subject fixed, the absentees are called in, and it is their business to interrogate the company seated round, one at a time, the object of the one being to discover the name of the man, and that of the other to ascertain the nature of the object. One question must be asked of each person in turn by each of the interrogators, and they must be questions which can be answered by a "yes" or "no." The first questions will naturally be "Is it a man?" "a woman?" "a child?" "living?" "dead?" "eighteenth century?" "later?" "earlier?" and so on. These questions narrow down the field of inquiry, and bring the interrogator nearer to the subject. In the meantime the questions as to the object will be interspersed, and these will naturally be, "Is it a manufactured article?" "a raw material?" "mineral?" "vegetable?" "animal?" etc., etc., etc. The two questioners may deal alternately with one person, or may take the company alternately, but they should not both question at the same time, as all the company are interested in hearing the cross-examination. The game proceeds until the puzzle is solved or the interrogators have to give it up.

Sherlock Holmes is a name suggested for a variation of the foregoing game by the *Evening News*. In this case the "detective" retires from the room, and the company concoct a crime which it is his business to detect. The crime suggested by this popular evening paper is as follows: "Shakespeare murdered Bacon, and threw his body into the River Avon." All these points are to be elicited in cross-examination in the manner already described. Other subjects of the same kind, but with a real basis in history, will readily occur to the reader. "The Murder of the Young Princes in the Tower," "The Execution of Mary Queen of Scots," "The Decapitation of Charles I.," etc., etc. Perhaps purely fictitious crimes like that attributed to Shakespeare in our first example are better adapted for mere amusement.

How, When, and Where is another *viva-voce* game, in which the company selects a subject which may be preferentially represented by a single word. The interrogators then proceed round the room, asking three questions, "How

do you like it ? " " When do you like it ? " and
" Where do you like it ? " and endeavouring to
guess the object from the answers given. A
simple and of course far too obvious example is
the following : " How do you like it ? " " Without milk." " When do you like it ? " " After
dinner." " Where do you like it ? " " At the
table," or " In the drawing-room." The obvious
answer to this is Coffee, but an enormous variety
of subjects may be chosen, representing every
degree of difficulty.

The Spelling Bee.—Spelling bees and roller
skates came into fashion about the same date,
and a wit of the time referred to them as symp-
toms of the " foot-and-mouth disease," an
ailment then prevalent among cattle. The
spelling bee " improved the shining hour," and
incidentally the national spelling for a while,
and then died a natural death. The roller skate
has grown in popularity; and in view of the
deterioration of the modern English winter,
appears to have come to stay. **The Spelling Bee**
in the first instance was a mere test of skill in
spelling, and it may still be used in its primary
form in entertaining young people—and all
people are young on festive occasions—with
interest, amusement, and profit, if prizes are
offered to those who survive the ordeal. If
played as a game at a private party the numbers
entering should be limited, or the game will
take too long. **The Interrogator,** who should
be appointed beforehand, should have a number
of words of graduated standards of difficulty
written down on paper, and taking the easier
words first should put them to the several
competitors in turn—a new word to each—who,
on failing to spell a word correctly, should leave
the group competing until the final round determines the winner or winners of the prizes.
The Progressive Spelling Bee adds to the study
of orthography a considerable exercise of ingenuity. The first player names a letter, and
each successive player adds a letter, with a view
to forming a word. The player who cannot
add a letter without completing a word loses the
game and pays a forfeit. An illustration of
this game was given some time ago in one of
the daily papers, which unfortunately the writer
is unable to name. In this five competitors were

supposed to take part, and the first-named the letter " S " to start the word. The second, third, and fourth players in turn added the letters " T," " I " and " F." This placed the fifth player in a quandary, for had he added a second " F " and completed the word STIFF, he would have lost the game and suffered forfeit. Happily, he thought of the letter " L," and so started the train of thought on to the line STIFLE. As only five competitors were playing, this would be a drawn game, unless the players had previously agreed to continue for a second round, or until such time as a word was completed. Had this been arranged, or had there been a larger number playing, the sixth player might have still escaped penalty by naming " I " and prolonging the word in the direction of STIFLING. The object is to postpone the naming of a letter which will make a complete word of those which preceded it, as long as possible, under penalty of a forfeit. This game is sometimes played under the name **Ghosts**, in which case three failures, which are called " lives," are allowed to each player before he becomes " dead " to the game. **Double Demon Spelling Bee** is a development of this game, and opens up larger opportunities of ingenuity by allowing prefixes as well as affixes. In this case each player has the option of adding his letter at either end of the word in process of formation, provided, of course, that he has in view a definite word, the correct spelling of which can be so promoted. Thus, continuing the illustration given above, the fifth player, fearing the letter " F," which would have completed the word STIFF, and not thinking of the letter " L," which diverted the word in the direction of the word STIFLE, might still have avoided forfeit had he thought of the prefix " A," which would have diverted the letters in the direction of the word MASTIFF. It will be seen that this game offers plenty of opportunity for ingenuity, and may sometimes be continued to considerable length. Prizes may be given in place of imposing forfeits, if those failing drop out of the competition one by one until only two are left. These should be judged equal.

Wills and Bequests.—In this game the

testator leaves the room, and the player who acts as lawyer writes down on a sheet of paper the various personal belongings of the testator as suggested by the company to the number of, say, twelve. These he will number in order, one to twelve. The list may include all sorts of absurd as well as sensible things, as the testator's motor-car, his fiancée, his mother-in-law, his temper, his debts, etc., etc., etc. The testator is then called into the room, and in ignorance of the nature and order of the bequests, is asked to whom he is desirous of leaving No. 1, No. 2, and so on, to the end. The names of the legatees are then written down by the side of the bequests, until the list is complete, and then the lawyer reads the will as nearly as possible in legal form. The amusement arises from the incongruity of the allocation of the odd bequests to the several legatees.

Clairvoyance, real or sham, always excites wonder, and the sham has the advantage of promoting amusement. The clairvoyant leaves the room, after taking a careful survey of its appointments and furniture. The professor then, speaking so that he may be heard by the clairvoyant through the closed door, says : " Do you remember the disposition of the various features of the room ? " to which the answer will be " Yes." The professor then proceeds to name various articles, suggested by the company (*sotto voce*), interrogatively, thus: "The piano ? " " Yes "; " The overmantel ? " " Yes "; " The clock ? " " Yes "; " And the coal-scuttle ? " " Yes "; " The settee ? " " Yes "; " The picture over the sideboard ? " " Yes," and so on, until a good number of articles have been named and acknowledged. The professor will then place his hand on the coal-scuttle and say : " Which of all these articles am I now touching with my hand ? " and the clairvoyant will immediately answer correctly. Why ? Because the professor used the word " and " before the word " coal-scuttle," and this gave the clue to his confidant. So long as the clue is understood beforehand it need not be used to apply to the word immediately following, but to the first, second, or third word after or before its introduction.

The Stool of Repentance is a game which often causes a great deal of amusement. The person who is to occupy the position retires from the room, and during his absence one, who is appointed spokesman, collects from the company, preferentially on paper, opinions or characterisations of the person in question. The absentee is then called in, and the opinions or characterisations are read to him one by one, and he is asked to guess who are the authors of the same. Failure to do so involves a forfeit. Within the limits of good taste, some very amusing opinions may be given and characterisations made, and all should be put to the occupier of the stool of repentance with some such formula as, " Deponent saith So-and-so. Who is your critic ? " These should be in the main real but amiable characterisations, but such opinions as : " Deponent saith You are no better than you ought to be," or, " You are never obstinate when you can have your own way," or " He would not trust you with his best girl," or " What you don't know, isn't worth knowing," etc., etc., etc., are admissible at discretion. This game gives a man's wife a chance not always open to her.

Games which have been called by various names, and which may be described as " **Message Games**," come under this category. The simplest form is that of a message or of a proverb which is whispered by the first player to the second, and by the second to the third, and so on, until it has completed the circle of the company. The fun of the game consists in the extraordinary difference which is found to exist between the original message and its final form. Each of the players should pass the message on with as much distinctness as possible, but should take care that it is not audible to any one but his immediate neighbour. In all games of this kind the original formula should be written down on paper, and kept in the possession of the first player, that it may be compared with its own mutilation at the finish of the round. If PROVERBS are used they should be such as are not too short, trite, or well known, though even these will seldom escape transformation in transmission. The following old proverbs may be suggestive : " Get thy spindle and thy distaff ready, and Heaven will send the flax." "He that hath a head of glass should not throw stones at another." "Better go to bed supperless than get up in debt," "It is wit to pick a lock and steal a horse, but it is wisdom to leave them alone." "They who would be young when they are old must be old when they are young." "Better ride on an ass with a sure foot than a horse that shies." If MESSAGES are sent they should be so framed that they may easily confuse the memory, but of course not so difficult as to spoil sport. The following formula which was proposed by Foote to Macklin as a test of memory, may be cited as an example of how to frame such a sentence, but of course in itself it is far too long for the purpose of this game. "So she went into the garden to cut a cabbage leaf to make an apple pie ; and at the same time a great she-bear coming up the street pops its head into the shop : 'What ! no soap ?' so he died, and she very imprudently married the barber ; and there were present the Piccaninnies and the Joblillies and the Garyulies and the great Panjandrum himself with the little round button on top ; and they all fell to playing the game of catch as catch can, till the gunpowder ran out at the heels of their boots."

Message Games may be made more complex and therefore more interesting, if they take the form of **A Telegram, reply paid.** In this game, which is played in the way already described, the abbreviated form of the telegraphic style lends itself to confusion and so to amusement ; and the interest is doubled when the message has completed its round, and a suitable reply is returned by the last player to the original sender by the same means. RUMOUR or GOSSIP is a name which may be given to another variation of this game. In this case some little piece of harmless scandal may form the sentence which is passed round. Yet another *viva-voce* game, in which whispers do not count, is one called **Shooting Proverbs.** In this two persons leave the room, and the company sitting round choose a proverb which in this case should be a fairly well known one, but not so long as to baffle solution. Supposing the proverb to be "It's a long lane that has no turning," the first player takes the word "it's," the second the word "a" the third the word "long," and so on until every word in the proverb is provided with a sponsor. If there are more guests than words, the proverb may be begun again, and continued as far as there are guests to represent it. When each guest is fitted with a word, the absentees are called in, and take their place in the centre of the room. The spokesman then calls out: "Make Ready! Present—Fire," and at the word "Fire" the whole company simultaneously shout the word of the proverb which has been allotted to them, and it is the object of the guessers to discover order in the babel of sounds. The guessers may call for the repetition of the shout with the same formula as often as they please, and they may walk round the room, and listen specially to individual voices to catch definite words as much as they like, until they have guessed the proverb or confessed their inability to do so. In most proverbs there are striking words which, once heard, give the game away. In the proverb cited above, the word "turning" would probably do this; in the proverb "a stitch in time saves nine," the word "stitch" would be an unfailing clue.

Paper Games. Games that require the use of pencil and paper, other than card games where the cards and pencils are procurable attached, involve some little trouble, as the want of a flat surface upon which to write often results in illegibility, and yet some of these games will well repay the trouble involved. **Pictures and Mottoes** is one of these. To play this game, pieces of paper folded across the middle are handed to each member of the company, and each is asked to write on one side of it the subject of a picture. This may be "The Coronation," "An Alpine Scene," "A Farm Yard," "A Storm at Sea," or any well-known picture, or any subject capable of pictorial treatment. When this is done each person refolds the paper concealing the subject written on the inside, and hands it to his right-hand neighbour, who, without opening it, writes a motto on the outside. These may be well-known proverbs, or lines, or couplets from poems, such as are often placed by artists beneath their pictures. This done, the papers should be handed to the next person on the right, who in turn should read out for the benefit of the company, first the subject, and then the motto. The result is not always congruous, but very often subjects and mottoes are found to be very suitably matched. The writer remembers several apposite examples which resulted in one game in which he took part. The picture, " A Farewell at a Railway Station," had for its motto " Oh ! for the touch of a vanished hand, and the sound of a voice that is still," and the picture " Cattle Grazing " bore the inscriptive motto " The nearer the bone, the sweeter the meat." In announcing the result it is sometimes found better to collect the papers immediately after the mottoes have been written, and hand them to some one to arrange, and give the readings in some appropriate order later on.

Adjectives is a name given to a game in which each player is supplied with a piece of paper, on which he is required to write several adjectives. These are collected by the principal player, who reads a page or two from some book, substituting, without regard to sense, the adjectives supplied by the players for those printed in the narrative. The result is both curious and amusing.

The Ancient Game of Crambo may still be included among parlour games. In this two pieces of paper, of different colour, are handed to each player, who is asked to write a noun on one colour and a question on the other. These papers are collected in separate hats, well mixed up, and again distributed. Each player has then to make up two or more lines of verse at once including the noun and answering the question. These are then collected and read out, for the general amusement.

The Game of Consequences is an old paper game which seems to enjoy perennial youth, and which with young people and at Christmastime, when the older games are commonly the most popular, can usually be trusted to cause general amusement. It is a " personal " game, and must be played with discretion, and strictly within the limits of good taste. A half-sheet of note paper is required by each player, who proceeds to write the name of a gentleman at the top. Each player then folds the paper to con-

ceal the name and hands it to his right-hand
neighbour. At the top of the paper as folded
each player then writes the name of a lady, folds
the paper again, and passes it on. Each player
then writes the name of a place, folds the paper,
and passes it on as before. What the gentleman
said is next inscribed, and after folding and
passing the paper, what the lady said; after
which what the gentleman did, and what the
lady did, are added separately in, and finally
the consequences finish up the story. When the
papers are completed, each player in turn, or
one appointed for the purpose, reads out the
results in the following formula : What's-his-
name met Mrs. or Miss So-and-so at such a
place. Mr. What's-his-name said this or that,
and Mrs. or Miss So-and-so said that or this.
Mr. What's-his-name then did thus-and-thus,
and Mrs. or Miss So-and-so said one thing or
another, and the consequences were ——
Though commonly the names of persons present,
or persons known to members of the company
are used in this game, those of public men and
women, historical persons, and characters in
fiction may often be used with great amusement.

Games at Forfeits commonly involving osculatory exercises are often popular with young
people at Christmas-time, and within the home
circle need not be disdained by their elders.
Usually the criers of forfeits fail in the variety
and suitability of the inflictions they impose,
and any one who would invent a number of new
penalties, which should be humorous without
being open to objection, would confer a benefit
and enable many games to be played which are
at present taboo. Many of the old ordeals are
somewhat trying. When a lady is condemned
to stand under the mistletoe and spell opportunity, she is asked to give an opportunity from
which she may not unnaturally shrink, and when
she is ordered to stand in the centre of the room
and repeat Nelson's famous signal at Trafalgar,
" England expects that every man this day will
do his duty," she really needs all the courage
of the combined fleets. That there are those to
whom such impositions would be really painful
is a sufficient reason why they should be applied
with discretion, and that, the blindfold conditions under which the penalties are dispensed

renders impossible. Under these circumstances it is best that only those should take part in these games who are prepared to accept the consequences. The writer well remembers being distressingly perturbed when, a small and bashful boy, he was ordered to " Bow to the wittiest, kneel to the prettiest, and kiss the girl he loved best in the room," and it was only when his mother pointed out to him how easy it was for him to discharge all his obligations at her feet that he rose to the occasion, and found, not for the first nor the last time, " a happy issue out of all his troubles " in her arms. Other osculatory penalties are " Kiss the four corners of the room," in which, of course, the lady is sure to find a gentleman ready to help her to redeem the behest ; " Kiss the flowers on the carpet," when the " weeds " will sometimes be found more numerous than the flowers ; " Measure six yards of love ribbon," effected by kneeling on cushions, face to face, with some chosen one joining hands in front, and then extending them sideways to their extreme limit, and thus bringing the lips together six times in succession, and " kissing rabbit fashion " brought about by nibbling rabbit fashion at the two ends of a piece of string until the lips meet and ratify the compact. A prettier forfeit of this kind may be borrowed from the " Valse Cotillion " and called, for this purpose, " The Mirror of Venus." In this case the lady sits with a mirror in one hand and a pocket-handkerchief in the other, while the gentlemen pass behind her chair and look in the mirror as they pass. One after one she essays to wipe the reflection out with her handkerchief, until she sees that of the face she chooses, when she looks up at the real face and—kisses meet.

THAT BABY

But exploiting worthy Whewell:—
Though his words were rather cruel—
When, in spite of pap and gruel,
    Baby cries.
When the early hours are creeping
And you're wakened from your sleeping,
If you wish to stop its weeping
    Dam its eyes.

A. H. M.

AT PARTING.

I. AULD LANG SYNE.

SHOULD auld acquaintance be forgot,
  And never brought to min' ?
Should auld acquaintance be forgot,
  And days o' lang syne ?

For auld lang syne, my dear,
  For auld lang syne,
We'll tak' a cup o' kindness yet,
  For auld lang syne.

And here's a hand, my trusty frien',
  And gie's a hand o' thine ;
And we'll tak' a right gude willie-waught
  For auld lang syne.

And surely ye'll be your pint stoup,
  And surely I'll be mine !
And we'll tak' a cup o' kindness yet,
  For auld lang syne.
    For auld lang syne, etc.

Willie-waught, draught ; *stoup*, measure.

II. GOD SAVE THE KING !

GOD save our gracious King,
Long live our noble King,
  God save the King !
Send him victorious,
Happy and glorious,
Long to reign over us,
  God save the King !

O Lord our God, arise,
Scatter his enemies,
  And make them fall !
Confound their politics,
Frustrate their knavish tricks
On Thee our hopes we fix—
  God save us all !

Thy choicest gifts in store,
On him be pleased to pour,
  Long may he reign !
May he defend our laws,
And ever give us cause
To sing, with heart and voice,
  God save the King.

ETIQUETTE.

SIR W. S. GILBERT

THE *Ballyshannon* foundered off the coast of
    Coriboo,
And down in fathoms many went the captain
    and his crew ;
Down with the owners, greedy men, whom hope
    of gain allured,
Oh, dry the starting tear—for they were heavily
    insured !

Beside the captain and the mate, the owners
    and the crew,
The passengers were also drowned excepting
    only two—
Young Peter Grey, who tasted teas for Baker,
    Croop & Co.,
And Somers, who from Eastern shores im-
    ported indigo.

These passengers, by reason of their clinging
    to a mast,
Upon a desert island were eventually cast.
They hunted for their meals, as Alexander
    Selkirk used,
But they couldn't chat together—they had not
    been introduced.

For Peter Grey, and Somers too, though certainly
    in trade,
Were properly particular about the friends they
    made ;
And somehow, thus they settled it, without a
    word of mouth,
That Grey should take the northern half, while
    Somers took the south.

On Peter's portion oysters grew, a delicacy rare,
But oysters were a delicacy Peter couldn't bear.
On Somers' side was turtle, on the shingle
    lying thick,
Which Somers couldn't eat, because it always
    made him sick.

Grey gnashed his teeth in envy, as he saw a
    mighty store
Of turtle, unmolested, on his fellow-creature's
    shore.

The oysters at his feet aside impatiently he
    shoved,
For turtle, and his mother, were the only things
    he loved.

And Somers sighed in sorrow, as he settled in
    the south,
For the thought of Peter's oysters brought the
    water to his mouth.
He longed to lay him down upon the shelly
    bed, and stuff,
For he'd often eaten oysters, but he'd never
    had enough.

How they wished an introduction to each other
    they had had,
When on board the *Ballyshannon*! and it
    almost drove them mad
To think how very friendly with each other
    they might get
If it wasn't for the arbitrary rule of etiquette.

One day when out a-hunting for the *mus-
    ridiculus*,
Grey overheard his fellow-man soliloquising
    thus :
" I wonder how the playmates of my youth
    are getting on—
McConnell, S. B. Walters, Paddy Byles, and
    Robinson ? "

These simple words made Peter as delighted
    as could be,
Old chummies at the Charter House were
    Robinson and he.
He walked straight up to Somers, then he turned
    extremely red,
Hesitated, hemmed and hawed, then cleared
    his throat and said :

" I beg your pardon—pray forgive me if I seem
    too bold—
But you have breathed a name I knew, familiarly
    of old.
You spoke aloud of Robinson—I happened to
    be by—
You know him ? " " Yes, extremely well."
    " Allow me—so do I."

It was enough—they felt they could more
    pleasantly get on,
For (oh! the magic of the fact) they each
    knew Robinson ;
And Mr. Somers' turtle was at Peter's service
    quite,
And Mr. Somers punished Peter's oyster-bed
    all right.

They soon became like brothers, from com-
    munity of wrongs,
They wrote each other little odes, and sang each
    other songs ;
They told each other anecdotes—disparaging
    their wives—
On several occasions too, they saved each other's
    lives.

They felt quite melancholy when they parted for
    the night,
And got up in the morning as soon as it was
    light.
Each other's pleasant company they reckoned
    so upon,
And all because it happened they each knew
    Robinson.

They lived for many years on that inhospitable
    shore,
And day by day they learned to love each other
    more and more.
At last, to their astonishment, on getting up one
    day,
They saw a frigate anchored in the offing of
    the bay.

To Peter an idea occurred—" Suppose we cross
    the main ?
So good an opportunity may not occur again."
And Somers thought a moment, then ejaculated,
    " Done !
I wonder how my business in the City's getting
    on ? "

" But stay ! " said Mr. Peter.   " When in Eng-
    land, as you know,
I earned a living tasting teas for Baker, Croop
    & Co.,

I may have been suspended—my employers
        think me dead,"
" Then come with me," said Somers, " and taste
        indigo instead."

But all their plans were scattered in a moment,
        when they found
The vessel was a convict ship from Portland,
        outward bound.
When a boat came out to fetch them, though
        they felt it very kind,
To go on board they firmly and respectfully
        declined.

As both the happy settlers roared with laughter
        at the joke
They recognised a gentlemanly fellow pulling
        stroke ;
'Twas *Robinson*, a convict, in an unbecoming
        frock,
Condemned to seven years' for misappropriating
        stock.

They laughed no more, for Somers thought he
        had been very rash
In knowing one whose friend had misappro-
        priated cash ;
And Peter thought a foolish tack he must have
        gone upon,
In making the acquaintance of a friend of
        Robinson.

At first they didn't quarrel very openly, I've
        heard ;
They nodded when they met, and now and then
        exchanged a word ;
The *word* grew rare, and rarer still the nodding
        of the head,
But when they meet each other *now*, they cut
        each other dead.

To allocate the Island they agreed by word of
        mouth,
And Peter takes the north again and Somers
        takes the south.
And Peter has the oysters, which he hates, in
        layers thick,
And Somers has the turtle, and it *always makes
        him sick*.

(By permission of Lady Gilbert.)

CORRECT DRESS.

OCCASION	COAT	WAISTCOAT	TROUSERS	HAT	SHIRT AND CUFFS	COLLAR	CRAVAT	GLOVES	SHOES	JEWELLERY
Day Wedding Afternoon Calls, Receptions and Matinée	Frock	Double Breasted Same Material as Coat or of White Linen Duck	Striped Worsted of Dark or Grey Tones	High Silk	White or Coloured with White Cuffs attached	Lap-Front or Point	Black, White or Light-tone Ascot or *Derby*	Grey Suede	Patent Leather	Gold Links, Pearl Pin
Evening Wedding, Balls, Receptions, Formal Dinners and Theatre	Evening Dress	White Double Breasted or Black Single Breasted	Same Material as Coat	Opera or High Silk	White with Cuffs attached	Lap-Front, Standing or Point	Broad End White Tie	Pearl or White	Patent Leather or Patent Leather Ties	Pearl Studs and White Links or Pearl Studs and Links
Informal Dinner, Club, and At-Home Dinner	Evening Jacket	Double Breasted White with Gold Buttons or S.B. Same Material as Coat	Same Material as Coat	*Black Alpine or Derby*	White with Cuffs attached	Standing or High-band Turn-down	Broad End Black Silk or Satin Tie	Grey Suede	Patent Leather or Patent Leather Ties	Gold Studs and Links

186

	Coat	Waistcoat	Trousers	Hat	Shirt	Collar	Tie	Gloves	Boots	Jewellery
Business and Morning Wear	Lounge, Morning or Frock	To Match Coat	If with S.B. Coat, to match; if with D.B. Coat, of some different Material	Derby with Sack or High Silk with Outaway	Coloured Shirt with Cuffs attached or separable	Standing or High-down Turn-down	Ascot Tie, Once-over or Derby	Tan or Grey	Calf with Sack; Patent Leather with Outaway	Gold Studs, Gold Links, Gold Watch Guard
Wheeling, Golf, Outing,	Single Breasted or Double Breasted Lounge	Of Fancy Plaid Single Breasted or Double Breasted	Fancy Knickers or Flannel Trousers	Alpine with Pugaree; Tam or Golf Cap	Fancy Flannel or Oxford	Hunting Stock or High-Band Turn-down or Neckerchief	Hunting Stock or Tie	Heavy Red Tan or White Chamois	Calf or Tan	Links and Watch Guard
Afternoon Teas, Shows, Etc.	Frock or Morning	Double Breasted Same Material as Coat or of White Linen Duck	Striped Worsted Light or Dark	High Silk	White	High Standing or Turn-down	Ascot or Derby	Tan or Light Grey Suede	Patent Leather	Gold Studs Gold Links

All Court Functions, Levees, Receptions, etc.—Special and very strict ancient regulations apply to these occasions, and it is necessary to consult one of the firms who are thoroughly aequainted with the rules and regulations.

COLLARS: "PELICAN" MAKE.

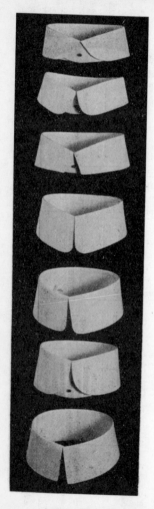

STADIUM.

2 in. back, 1¼ in. front.

ST. ANDREWS.

1¾ in. and 2 in.

SQUARE STADIUM.

2 in. back, 1¼ in front.

THE "CINCH."

2 in. and 2¼ in.

Also in Quarter Sizes.

BADEN-POWELL.

2 in., 2¼ in. and 2½ in.

Also in Quarter Sizes.

BURLINGTON.

2 in., 2¼ in. and 2½ in.

SQUARE "CINCH."

2 in. and 2¼ in.

COLLARS: "PELICAN" MAKE.

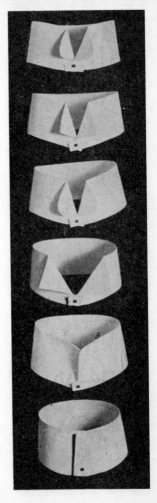

MAYFAIR.

2 in., 2¼ in. and 2½ in.

Also in Quarter Sizes.

SQUARE MAYFAIR.

2¼ in. and 2½ in.

WING.

2¼ in. and 2½ in.

NOBILITY.

Full 2 in.

FITZWILLIAM.

2¼ in., 2½ in. and 2¾ in.

STANHOPE.

2¼ in., 2½ in. and 2¾ in.

THE OXFORD TIE.

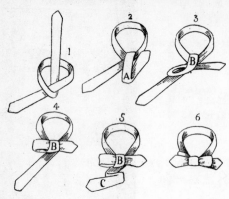

THE ASCOT TIE.

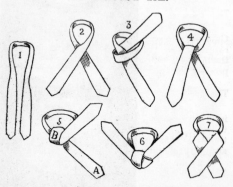

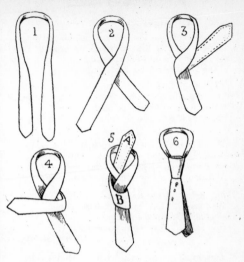

From designs by N. T. Greenlaw & Co., by permission.

THE CORRECT WAY TO TIE NECKWEAR.

The Oxford Tie.

The diagram shows a new way of tying the Oxford Tie into a straight bow: Fold A with reversing turn to form the loop B (fig. 3 is a half turn), then fold C and pass through loop B to produce fig. 6 (fig. 4 is a complete turn).

The Ascot Tie.

This diagram shows the tying of the Ascot Tie into a pin shape. The advantage of this tie is that both ends can be used in tying: Pass A through B, drop ends down to produce fig. 7, and pin is required.

The Four-in-Hand Scarf.

The diagram shows the tying of the Four-in-Hand Scarf into a sailor's knot: Pass A through B to produce fig.

LOVE AND KISSES.

THEIR sweet salutes are not misplaced
　　When women kiss a friend or brother,
But surely 'tis a wicked waste
　　When women kiss each other.

And yet a Christian virtue they may teach,
With greater eloquence than parsons preach,
By doing unto others as they would
That *men* should do to them, and that is good.
　　　　　　　　　　　　　　　　　　M.

"May I print a kiss on your lips ?" I said,
　　And she nodded her sweet permission ;
So we went to press, and I rather guess
　　We printed a big edition.—*Modern Society.*

HE met her in the darkened hall
　　And said, "I've brought some roses."
Her answer seemed irrelevant,
　　She said, "How cold your nose is !"
　　　　　　　　　　　Modern Society.

"You must give back," her mother said
To the poor sobbing little maid,
"All the young man has given you,
Hard as it now may seem to do."
"'Tis done already, mother dear,"
Said the sweet girl, "so never fear,
All the fond looks and words that passed
And all the kisses to the last."—*W. P. Landor.*

The old world was a pleasant place
　　Before the scientist
Brought men and microbes face to face
　　And bade the man resist.
A pretty girl I may not kiss,
　　Lest evil germs escape her,
And put an end to all my bliss—
　　For life is but a vapour ?
Though heart should fail and senses whirl,
　　And 'twere my final dinner,
I'd rather eat the pretty girl
　　And all the microbes in her.—*A. H. M.*

"Go ask papa," the maiden said.
He, knowing her papa was dead,
And what a wicked life he'd led,
Quite understood her, when she said,
　　"Go ask papa."

MARRIAGE

Marriages are made in heaven.

Marriage and hanging go by destiny.

Two untied are drawn together,
Tie them and they strain the tether.—*M.*

Who woo in poetry may wed in prose,
And tragedy may bring the farce to close.—*M.*

Let me not to the marriage of true minds
Admit impediments.— *Shakespeare.*

Wed-lock without love, they say,
Is like a lock without a key.—*Butler.*

Yet some have found who long have tarried,
There are worse things than getting married.—*M.*

They were so one that none could ever say,
Which most did rule, and which did most obey.
He ruled because she would obey, and she,
In the obeying, ruled as much as he.

He paid her compliments of yore,
   And now he pays her bills,
And time runs up a pretty score,
   For homely joys and ills ;
But when the times are wintriest,
   To show she only borrows,
She pays him back with interest
   In all his joys and sorrows.

The honey-moon is very strange.
Unlike all other moons the change
   She regularly undergoes :
She rises at the full ; then loses
Much of her brightness ; then reposes
   Faintly ; and then . . . has naught to lose.
                        W. S. Landor.

All moons for ever wax and wane,
Who will, may watch, nor watch in vain,
The faintest round to full again.—*M.*

A hundred times I softly sighed,
   "Be mine, dear maid, be mine,"
Ere she consented. Now I wish
   I'd stopped at ninety-nine.—*W. Thomson.*

I loved thee, beautiful and kind,
  And plighted an eternal vow;
So altered are thy face and mind,
  'Twere perjury to love thee now.
                    Lord Nugent.

When man and wife at odds fall out,
  Let syntax be your tutor:
'Twixt masculine and feminine
  What should we be but neuter?

"How like is my picture, the pose of the head,
  The life, the expression, the spirit!
It wants but a tongue!" "Oh no, dear," he said,
  "That want is its principal merit."

Brown lisps, and says that for a whole long
He has not spoken to his lady "wonth." [month
"A bear," you call him? Nay, not so abrupt, sir,
He's too polite—he will not interrupt her.—*M.*

"My love, you never kiss me
  Unless you want some money;
It seems that you in this do
  Much like the bee and honey."
"But surely, darling, that's no cause for
    huff,
You ought to find my kisses quantum suff.
Am I not wanting money oft enough?"—*M.*

"My dear, what makes you always yawn?"
  The wife exclaimed, her temper gone.
    "Is home so dull and dreary?"
"Not so, my love," he said, "not so,
But man and wife are one, you know,
  And when alone I'm weary."

"Come hither, Sir John, my picture is here,
  What say you, my love, does it strike you?"
"I can't say it does, just at present, my dear,
  But I think it soon will, it's so like you."

"Lo! here's the bride and there's the tree,
  Take which of these best liketh thee."
"The bargain's bad on either part,
  But, hangman, come, drive on the cart."

FORTUNE

Who of the maidens I have seen
    Should I the last importune ?
Though the most constant—she has been
      Miss Fortune.

What dame—were I to challenge Fate
    By marrying another—
Should I with least misgiving mate—
    Her mother ?—*M.*

They may talk as they please about what they
    call pelf,
And how one ought never to think of oneself,
How pleasures of thought surpass eating and
    drinking ;
My pleasure of thought is the pleasure of
    thinking.
    How pleasant it is to have money, heigh-ho !
    So pleasant it is to have money.

It's all very well to be handsome and tall,
Which certainly makes you look well at a ball ;
It's all very well to be clever and witty,
But if you are poor, why it's only a pity.
    So needful it is to have money, heigh-ho !
    So needful it is to have money.

There's something undoubtedly in a fine air,
To know how to smile and be able to stare ;
High breeding is something, but well-bred or not,
In the end the one question is, what have you
    got ?
    So needful it is to have money, heigh-ho !
    So needful it is to have money.
                A. H. Clough.

Good Luck is the gayest of all gay girls ;
    Long in one place she will not stay :
Back from your brow she strokes the curls,
    Kisses you quick and flies away.

But Madame Bad Luck soberly comes
    And stays—no fancy has she for flitting—
Snatches of true-love songs she hums,
    And sits by your bed, and brings her
      knitting.—*John Hay*

It's when a man would borrow
    That he is brought to see,
And find out, to his sorrow,
    How close a friend can be.—*Anon.*

His velvet-like paws hide his talons of steel,
He smiles as he thinks how you'll break on his
    wheel ;
He'll smile at your wit and he'll humour your
    bent,
The price of his friendship three hundred per
    cent.

" He owned a million yesterday,"
    They said—said one who'd known him :
" Was ever millionaire could say
    His money didn't own *him* ?

A self-made man who boasts his own ability
Relieves God of a great responsibility.

Once I pictured, fondly yearning,
    All the gay and merry sport
That would greet my ship returning
        Into port.
Now I crow a very low note,
    And 'twill be a modest din
That will greet my little row-boat
        Coming in.

"Life is short ! " the preacher cried
    From the pulpit up on high.
Jameson heard and softly sighed :
"True ! ah, true ! And so am I."

"Life is real ! " the preacher said.
    Jameson nodded.   Vain regrets !
Bowed in patience he his head,
    " So," he sighed, " are all my debts."

"Life is earnest ! " next he heard.
    Cold sweat oozed through all his pores.
" Yes," he whispered, " that's the word :
So are all my creditors."—*Tribune.*

A hope fulfilled in perfect bliss
    Has been of many a tale the text ;
How false of life, unless it is
    " To be continued in our next."

THE LAWS OF WHIST

(Reprinted, by permission, from the Revised Code, 1900.)

CARDS

1. Two packs of cards are used, one being used by each side.

2. A card or cards torn or marked must be either replaced by agreement, or new cards called for at the expense of the table.

3. Any player, before the pack is cut for the deal, may call for fresh cards on paying for them. He must call for two new packs, of which the dealer takes his choice.

CUTTING OR DRAWING

4. The ace is the lowest card in cutting or drawing.

5. In all cases, every one must cut or draw from the same pack.

6. Should a player expose or draw more than one card, he must cut or draw again.

FORMATION OF TABLE

7. (a) The candidates first in the room have the preference. When there are more than six candidates, and there is a doubt or question as to the preference of two or more of them, they determine their preference by drawing. Those drawing the lower cards have the preference. The table is complete with six players. On the retirement of any of those six players, the candidates who, in the first draw, drew the lowest cards have the prior right to enter the table.

(b) If there are more than four players they all draw, and the four who draw the lowest cards play first.

(c) When two or more candidates or players draw cards of equal value they draw again, if necessary, to determine their precedence.

PARTNERS

8. The four who play first again draw to decide on partners. The two lowest play against the two highest. The lowest is the dealer and

has choice of cards and seats, and, having once made his selection, must abide by it.

9. Two players drawing cards of equal value, which are not the two highest, draw again. If the equal cards are not the two lowest, the higher in the new draw plays with the highest in the original draw ; if the equal cards are the two lowest, the new draw decides who is to deal.[1]

[1] *Example.* A three, two sixes, and a knave are drawn. The two sixes draw again, and the lower plays with the three. Suppose, at the second draw, the two sixes draw a king and a queen, the queen plays with the three.

If at the second draw, a lower card than the three is drawn the three still retains its privileges as original low, and has the deal and choice of cards and seats.

10. Three players drawing cards of equal value draw again ; should the fourth (or remaining) card be the highest in the original draw, the two lowest of the new draw are partners, the lower of those two the dealer ; should the fourth card be the lowest, the two highest are partners, the original lowest the dealer.[2]

[2] *Example.* Three aces and a two are drawn. The three aces draw again. The two is the original high, and plays with the highest of the next draw.

Suppose, at the second draw, two more twos and a king are drawn. The king plays with the original two, and the other pair of twos draw again for deal.

Suppose, instead, the second draw to consist of an ace and two knaves. The two knaves draw again, and the higher plays with the two.

CUTTING OUT

11. At the end of a rubber, should admission be claimed by any one, or by two candidates, he who has, or they who have, played a greater number of consecutive rubbers than the other is, or are, out ; but when two or more have played the same number, they must, when necessary, cut or draw to decide upon the outgoers ; the highest are out.

ENTRY AND RE-ENTRY

12. A candidate wishing to enter a table must declare such intention prior to any of the players having drawn a card, either for the purpose of commencing a fresh rubber or of cutting into.

12 *a.* Any candidate may declare into any table that is not complete. If he do so he shall have priority over any candidate who has not previously declared in.

13. In the formation of fresh tables, those candidates who have not played at any other table have the prior right of entry ; the others decide their right of admission by drawing.

14. Any one quitting a table prior to the conclusion of a rubber may, with consent of the other three players, appoint a substitute in his absence during that rubber.

15. A player cutting into one table, whilst belonging to another, loses his prior right of re-entry into that latter, and takes his chance of cutting in, as if he were a fresh candidate, and last in the room.

16. If any one break up a table, the remaining players have the prior right to him of entry into any other, and should there not be sufficient vacancies at such other table to admit all those candidates, they settle their precedence by drawing.

SHUFFLING

17. After the selection of cards for the first deal has been made, it is the duty of an adversary to shuffle the pack selected, and of the player who is about to deal, or of his partner, to shuffle the other pack.

18. The pack must neither be shuffled below the table, nor so that the face of any card be seen.

19. The pack must not be shuffled during the play of the hand.

20. A pack, having been played with, must not be shuffled by dealing it into packets.

21. Each player has a right to shuffle once only, except as provided by Law 24, prior to a deal, after a false cut,[1] or prior to a new deal.[2]

22. The dealer's partner must collect the cards for the ensuing deal, and has the first right to shuffle that pack.

23. Each player, after shuffling, must place the cards, properly collected and face downwards, to the left of the player about to deal them.

24. The dealer has always the right to shuffle last. Should a card or cards be seen during his shuffling or whilst giving the pack to be cut, he may be compelled to re-shuffle.

Vide Law 26.   [2] *Vide* Law 29.

The Deal

25. The deal commences with the player who cut the original lowest card, the next deal falls to the player on his left, and so on until the rubber is finished.

26. When the pack has been finally shuffled, the player about to deal shall present it to the adversary on his right, who shall cut it, and in dividing it, must not leave fewer than four cards in either packet; if in cutting, or in replacing one of the two packets on the other, a card be exposed,[1] or if there be any confusion of the cards, or a doubt as to the exact place in which the pack was divided, there must be a fresh cut.

27. When the player whose duty it is to cut has once separated the pack, he cannot alter his intentions; he can neither re-shuffle nor re-cut the cards.

28. When the pack is cut, should the dealer shuffle the cards, he loses his deal.

29. There must be a new deal by the same dealer [2]—

   I. If, during a deal, or during the play of a hand, the pack be proved incorrect or imperfect.

   II. If any card, excepting the last, be faced in the pack.

   III. If a player takes up another player's hand.

30. If, whilst dealing, a card be exposed on or below the table by the dealer or his partner, should neither of the adversaries have touched the cards, the latter can claim a new deal; a card exposed by either adversary gives that claim to the dealer, provided that his partner has not touched a card; if a new deal does not take place, the exposed card cannot be called.

31. If, during dealing, a player touch any of his cards, the adversaries may do the same, without losing their privilege of claiming a new deal, should chance give them such option.

32. If, in dealing, one of the cards be exposed, and the dealer turn up the trump before there is reasonable time for his adversaries to decide as

[1] After the two packets have been re-united, Law 30 comes into operation.

[2] *Vide* also Laws 36 and 41.

to a fresh deal, they do not thereby lose their privilege.

33. If a player, whilst dealing, look at the trump card, his adversaries have a right to see it, and either may exact a new deal.

34. Any one dealing out of turn, or with the adversary's cards, may be stopped before the trump card is turned up, after which the game must proceed as if no mistake had been made.

35. A player can neither shuffle, cut, nor deal for his partner, without the permission of his opponents.

36. If the adversaries interrupt a dealer whilst dealing, either by questioning the score or asserting that it is not his deal, and fail to establish such claim, should a misdeal occur, he may deal again.

A Misdeal

37. It is a misdeal [1]—

   I. Unless the cards are dealt into four packets, one at a time in regular rotation, beginning with the player to the dealer's left.

   II. Should the dealer place the last (which is called the trump) card, face downwards, on his own or on any other packet.

   III. Should the trump card not come in its regular order to the dealer; but he does not lose his deal if the pack be proved imperfect.

   IV. Should a player have fourteen or more cards, and any of the other three less than thirteen; [2] unless the excess has arisen through the act of an adversary, in which case there must be a fresh deal.

   V. Should the dealer touch, for the purpose of counting, the cards on the table or the remainder of the pack.

   VI. Should the dealer deal two cards at once, or two cards to the same hand, and then deal a third; but if, prior to dealing that third card, the dealer can, by altering the position of one card

---

1 *Vide* also Law 28.
2 The pack being perfect. *Vide* Law 41.

only, rectify such error, he may do so,
except as provided by the second
paragraph of this Law.

VII. Should the dealer omit to have the pack
cut to him, and the adversaries discover the error, prior to the trump
card being turned up, and before
looking at their cards, but not after
having done so.

38. Should a player take his partner's deal,
and misdeal, the latter is liable to the usual
penalty, and the adversary next in rotation to
the player who ought to have dealt then deals.

39. A misdeal loses the deal;[1] unless, during
the dealing, either of the adversaries touch the
cards prior to the dealer's partner having done
so; but should the latter have first interfered
with the cards, notwithstanding either or both
of the adversaries have subsequently done the
same, the deal is lost.

40. Should three players have their right
number of cards—the fourth have less than
thirteen, and not discover such deficiency until
the first trick has been turned and quitted, the
pack shall be assumed to be complete, and the
deal stands good; and he will be answerable for
any revoke he may have made, in the same way
as if the missing card or cards had been in his
hand.

41. If a pack, during or after a rubber, be
proved incorrect or imperfect, such proof does
not alter any past score, game, or rubber; that
hand in which the imperfection was detected
is null and void (except in the case of such
deficiency as is provided for by Law 40); the
dealer deals again.

The Trump Card

42. The dealer, when it is his turn to play to
the first trick, should take the trump card into
his hand; if left on the table after the second
trick be turned and quitted, it is liable to be
called.[2] His partner may at any time remind
him of the liability.

43. After the dealer has taken the trump card
into his hand, it must not be asked for; a player

---

[1] Except as provided in Law 36.
[2] It is not usual to call the trump card if left on the table.

naming it at any time during the play of that
hand is liable to have his highest or lowest
trump called. Such call cannot be repeated.
Any player may at any time inquire what the
trump suit is.

44. If the dealer take the trump card into his
hand before it is his turn to play, he may be
desired to lay it on the table; should he show
a wrong card, this card may be called, as also a
second, a third, etc., until the trump card be
produced.

45. If the dealer declare himself unable to
recollect the trump card, his highest or lowest
trump may be called at any time during that
hand, and, unless it cause him to revoke, must
be played; the call may be repeated, but not
changed (*i.e.* from highest to lowest, or *vice
versa*) until such card is played.

THE RUBBER

46. The rubber is the best of three games.
If the first two games be won by the same
players, the third game is not played.

SCORING

47. A game consists of five points. Each
trick, above six, counts one point.

48. Honours, *i.e.* Ace, King, Queen, and
Knave of trumps, are thus reckoned:

If a player and his partner, either separately
or conjointly, hold—

I. The four honours, they score four points.

II. Any three honours, they score two points.

49. Those players who, at the commencement
of a deal, are at the score of four, cannot score
honours.

50. The penalty for a revoke [1] takes precedence
of all other scores. Tricks score next. Honours
last.

51. Honours, unless claimed before the trump
card of the following deal is turned up, cannot
be scored.

52. To score honours is not sufficient; they
must be claimed at the end of the hand; if so
claimed, they may be scored at any time during
the game. If the tricks won, added to honours

[1] *Vide* Law 75.

held, suffice to make game, it is sufficient to call game.

53. The winners gain—

    I. A treble, or game of three points, when their adversaries have not scored.

    II. A double, or game of two points, when their adversaries have scored one or two.

    III. A single, or game of one point, when their adversaries have scored three or four.

54. The winners of the rubber gain two points (commonly called the rubber points) in addition to the value of their games.

55. Should the rubber have consisted of three games, the value of the losers' game is deducted from the gross number of points gained by their opponents.

56. If an erroneous score be proved, such mistake can be corrected prior to the conclusion of the game in which it occurred, and such game is not concluded until the trump card of the following deal has been turned up.

57. If an erroneous score, affecting the value of the rubber,[1] be proved, such mistake can be rectified at any time during the rubber.

Cards Liable to be Called

58. The following are exposed cards :—

    I. Two or more cards played at once, face upwards.

    II. Any card dropped with its face upwards, in any way on or above the table, even though snatched up so quickly that no one can name it.

    III. Every card named by the player holding it.

59. All exposed cards are liable to be called, and must be left or placed face upwards on the table. If two or more cards are played at once, the adversaries have a right to call which they please to the trick in course of play, and afterwards to call the remainder. A card is not an exposed card, under the preceding Law, when dropped on the floor, or elsewhere below the table. An adversary may not require any exposed card to be played before it is the turn of the owner

---

[1] *E.g.* If a single is scored by mistake for a double or treble, or *vice versa.*

of the card to play; should he do so, he loses his right to exact the penalty for that trick.

60. If any one play to an imperfect trick the winning card on the table, and then lead without waiting for his partner to play, or lead one which is a winning card as against his adversaries, and then lead again, without waiting for his partner to play, or play several such winning cards, one after the other, without waiting for his partner to play, the latter may be called on to win, if he can, the first or any other of those tricks, and the subsequent cards thus improperly played are exposed cards.

61. If a player or players (not being all) throw his or their cards on the table face upwards, such cards are exposed, and liable to be called, each player's by the adversary; but no player who retains his hand can be forced to abandon it.

62. If all four players throw their cards on the table face upwards, the hands are abandoned; and no one can again take up his cards. Should this general exhibition show that the game might have been saved or won by the losers, neither claim can be entertained unless a revoke be established. The revoking players are then liable to the following penalties: they cannot under any circumstances win the game by the result of that hand, and the adversaries may add three to their score, or deduct three from that of the revoking players, for each revoke.

63. If a card be detached from the rest of the hand, which an adversary at once correctly names, such card becomes an exposed card; but should the adversary name a wrong card, he is liable to have a suit called when he or his partner next have the lead.

64. If any player lead out of turn, his adversaries may either call the card erroneously led, or may call a suit from him or his partner when it is next the turn of either of them to lead. The penalty of calling a suit must be exacted from whichever of them next first obtains the lead. It follows that if the player who leads out of turn is the partner of the person who ought to have led, and a suit is called, it must be called at once from the right leader. If he is allowed to play as he pleases, the only penalty that remains is to call the card erroneously led. The fact that the card erroneously

led has been played without having been called,
does not deprive the adversaries of their right
to call a suit. If a suit is called, the card erroneously led may be replaced in the owner's hand.

65. If it is one player's lead, and he and his
partner lead simultaneously, the penalty of
calling the highest or lowest card of the suit
properly led may be exacted from the player
in error, or the card simultaneously led may be
treated as a card liable to be called.

66. If any player lead out of turn, and the
other three have followed him, the trick is complete, and the error cannot be rectified; but if
only the second, or the second and third, have
played to the false lead, their cards, on discovery of the mistake, are taken back; there is
no penalty against any one, excepting the original
offender, whose card may be called—or he, or
his partner (whichever of them next first has the
lead), may be compelled to play any suit demanded by the adversaries.

67. In no case can a player be compelled to
play a card which would oblige him to revoke.

68. The call of a card may be repeated at
every trick, until such card has been played.

69. If a player called on to lead a suit have
none of it, the penalty is paid.

Irregular Play

70. If the third hand play before the second,
the fourth hand may play before his partner.

71. Should the third hand not have played,
and the fourth play before his partner, the
latter may be called on to win or not to win the
trick.

72. If any one omit playing to a trick, and
such error be not discovered until he has played
to the next, the adversaries may claim a new
deal; should they decide that the deal stand
good, the surplus card at the end of the hand is
considered to have been played to the imperfect
trick, but does not constitute a revoke therein.

73. If any one play two cards to the same
trick, or mix his trump, or other card, with a
trick to which it does not properly belong, and
the mistake be not discovered until the hand is
played out, he is answerable for all consequent
revokes he may have made.[1] If, during the

Vide also Law 40.

play of the hand, the error be detected, the
tricks may be counted face downwards, in order
to ascertain whether there be among them a
card too many; should this be the case they
may be searched, and the card restored; the
player is, however, liable for all revokes which
he may have meanwhile made. If no revoke
has been made, the card can be treated as an
exposed card.

THE REVOKE

74. It is a revoke when a player, holding one
or more cards of the suit led, plays a card of a
different suit.

75. The penalty for a revoke—

  I. Is at the option of the adversaries, who,
      at the end of the hand, may either
      take three tricks from the revoking
      player and add them to their own
      tricks, or deduct three points from his
      score, or add three to their own score
      (the adversaries may consult as to
      which penalty they will exact);

 II. Can be claimed for as many revokes as
      occur during the hand, and a different
      penalty may be exacted for each
      revoke;

III. Is applicable only to the score of the
      game in which it occurs;

 IV. Cannot be divided, i.e. a player cannot
      add one or two to his own score, and
      deduct one or two from the revoking
      player;

  V. Takes precedence of every other score—
      e.g. The claimants two—their oppo-
      nents nothing—the former add three
      to their score—and thereby win a
      treble game, even should the latter
      have made thirteen tricks, and held
      four honours.

76. If a player who has become liable to have
the highest or lowest of a suit called, or to win
or not to win a trick (when able to do so), fail
to play as desired, or if a player, when called
on to lead one suit, lead another, having in his
hand one or more cards of that suit demanded,
he incurs the penalty of a revoke.

77. A revoke is established, if the trick in

which it occur be turned and quitted, *i.e.* the hand removed from that trick after it has been turned face downwards on the table—or if either the revoking player or his partner, whether in his right turn or otherwise, lead or play to the following trick. Throwing down the hand, or claiming game, constitute acts of play within the meaning of leading or playing to the following trick.

78. A player may ask his partner whether he has not a card of the suit which he has renounced, or whether he has played as desired or demanded. Should the question be asked before the trick is turned and quitted, subsequent turning and quitting by the adversaries does not establish the revoke, and the error may be corrected, unless the question be answered in the negative, or unless the revoking player or his partner have led or played to the following trick ; but if the revoking player or his partner has turned the trick before the question is answered, the revoke is established.

79. At the end of a hand, the claimants of a revoke may search all the tricks.[1]

80. If a player discover his error in time to save a revoke, the adversaries, whenever they think fit, may call the card thus played in error, or may require him to play his highest or lowest card to that trick in which he has renounced ; —any player or players who have played after him may withdraw their cards and substitute others ; the cards withdrawn are not liable to be called.

81. If a revoke be claimed, and the accused player or his partner, after such claim has been made, mix the cards before they have been sufficiently examined by the adversaries, the revoke is established. Prior to such claim, the mixing of the cards renders the proof of a revoke difficult, but does not prevent the claim, and possible establishment, of the penalty.

82. A revoke cannot be claimed after the cards have been duly cut for the following deal.

83. The revoking player and his partner may, under all circumstances, require the hand in which the revoke has been detected to be played out.

84. If a revoke occur, be claimed and proved,

1 *Vide* Law 81.

bets on the odd trick, or on amount of score, must be decided by the actual state of the latter, after the penalty is paid.

85. Should the players on both sides subject themselves to the penalty of one or more revokes, neither can win the game, and the revokes cancel each other.

86. In whatever way the penalty be enforced, under no circumstances can a player win the game by the result of the hand during which he has revoked; he cannot score more than four.

EXACTION OF PENALTIES

87. Where a player and his partner have an option of exacting from their adversaries one of two penalties, they must agree who is to make the election, and mnst not consult with one another which of the two penalties it is advisable to exact; if they do so consult, they lose their right to demand any penalty; and if either of them, with or without consent of his partner, demand a penalty to which he is entitled, such decision is final.

This rule does not apply in exacting the penalties for a revoke; partners have then a right to consult.

88. Any player demanding a penalty which is not authorised for the offence committed, forfeits all right to exact any penalty for the offence in question.

GENERAL RULES

89. Any one during the play of a trick, or after the four cards are played, and before, but not after, they are touched for the purpose of gathering them together, may demand that the cards be placed before their respective players.

90. If any one, prior to his partner playing, should call attention to the trick—either by saying that it is his, or by naming his card, or, without being required so to do, by drawing it toward him—the adversaries may require that opponent's partner to play the highest or lowest of the suit then led, or to win or not to win the trick.

91. In all cases where a penalty has been incurred, the offender is bound to give reasonable time for the decision of his adversaries.

92. If a bystander make any remark, before the stakes have been paid, which calls the attention of a player or players to an oversight affecting the score, he is liable to be called on, by the players only, to pay the stakes and all bets on that game or rubber.

93. A bystander, by agreement among the players, may decide any question.

94. When a trick has been turned and quitted, it must not again be looked at until the hand has been played out, except as provided by Law 73. A violation of this Law renders the offender, or his partner, liable to have a suit called when it is the next turn of either of them to lead.

DUMMY

Is played by three players.

One hand, called Dummy's, lies exposed on the table.

The Laws are the same as those of Whist, with the following exceptions :—

1. Dummy deals at the commencement of each rubber.

2. Dummy is not liable to the penalty for a revoke, as his adversaries see his cards. Should he revoke, and the error not be discovered until the trick is turned and quitted, it stands good. If Dummy's partner revokes, he is liable to the usual penalties.

3. There is no misdeal.

4. Dummy being blind, and deaf, his partner is not liable to any penalty for an error whence he can gain no advantage. Thus he may expose some or all of his cards, or declare that he has the game or trick, etc., without incurring any penalty; if, however, he lead from Dummy's hand when he should lead from his own, or *vice versa*, a suit may be called from the hand which ought to have led.

DOUBLE DUMMY

Is played by two players, each having a Dummy or exposed hand for his partner.

The Laws of the game do not differ from those of Dummy Whist.

THE LAWS OF BRIDGE

(As Revised by the Portland and Turf Clubs, 1904)

REPRINTED, BY PERMISSION, *VERBATIM* FROM
THE CLUB CODE.

Printed by kind permission of THOMAS DE LA RUE & CO.
LIMITED, *London.*

THE RUBBER

1. The Rubber is the best of three games.
If the first two games be won by the same
players, the third game is not played.

SCORING

2. A game consists of thirty points obtained
by tricks alone, exclusive of any points counted
for Honours, Chicane, or Slam.

3. Every hand is played out, and any points
in excess of the thirty points necessary for the
game are counted.

4. Each trick above six counts two points
when spades are trumps, four points when clubs
are trumps, six points when diamonds are
trumps, eight points when hearts are trumps,
and twelve points when there are no trumps.

5. Honours consist of ace, king, queen, knave,
and ten of the trump suit. When there are no
trumps they consist of the four aces.

6. Honours in trumps are thus reckoned :
If a player and his partner conjointly hold—

   I. The five honours of the trump suit, they
       score for honours five times the value
       of the trump suit trick.

  II. Any four honours of the trump suit, they
       score for honours four times the value
       of the trump suit trick.

III. Any three honours of the trump suit, they
       score for honours twice the value of the
       trump suit trick.

If a player in his own hand holds—

   I. The five honours of the trump suit, he and
       his partner score for honours ten times
       the value of the trump suit trick.

  II. Any four honours of the trump suit,
       they score for honours eight times the
       value of the trump suit trick. In this

last case, it the player's partner holds the fifth honour, they also score for honours the single value of the trump suit trick.

The value of the trump suit trick referred to in this law is its original value—*e.g.* two points in spades and six points in diamonds ; and the value of honours is in no way affected by any doubling or re-doubling that may take place under Laws 53–60.

7. HONOURS, when there are no trumps, are thus reckoned :

If a player and his partner conjointly hold—

> I. The four aces, they score for honours forty points.

> II. Any three aces, they score for honours thirty points.

If a player in his own hand holds—

> The four aces, he and his partner score for honours one hundred points.

8. CHICANE is thus reckoned :

> If a player holds no trump, he and his partner score for Chicane twice the value of the trump suit trick. The value of Chicane is in no way affected by any doubling or re-doubling that may take place under Laws 53–60.

9. SLAM is thus reckoned :

If a player and his partner make, independently of any tricks taken for the revoke penalty—

> I. All thirteen tricks, they score for Grand Slam forty points.

> II. Twelve tricks, they score for Little Slam twenty points.

10. Honours, Chicane, and Slam are reckoned in the score at the end of the rubber.

11. At the end of the rubber, the total scores for tricks, honours, Chicane, and Slam obtained by each player and his partner are added up, one hundred points are added to the score of the winners of the rubber, and the difference between the two scores is the number of points won, or lost, by the winners of the rubber.

12. If an erroneous score affecting tricks be proved, such mistake may be corrected prior to the conclusion of the game in which it occurred, and such game is not concluded until the last card of the following deal has been dealt, or, in the case of the last game of the rubber, until the score has been made up and agreed.

13. If an erroneous score affecting honours, Chicane, or Slam be proved, such mistake may be corrected at any time before the score of the rubber has been made up and agreed.

CUTTING

14. The ace is the lowest card.

15. In all cases, every player must cut from the same pack.

16. Should a player expose more than one card, he must cut again.

FORMATION OF TABLE

17. If there are more than four candidates, the players are selected by cutting, those first in the room having the preference. The four who cut the lowest cards play first, and again cut to decide on partners ; the two lowest play against the two highest ; the lowest is the dealer, who has choice of cards and seats, and, having once made his selection, must abide by it.

18. When there are more than six candidates, those who cut the two next lowest cards belong to the table, which is complete with six players ; on the retirement of one of those six players, the candidate who cut the next lowest card has a prior right to any after-comer to enter the table.

19. Two players cutting cards of equal value, unless such cards are the two highest, cut again ; should they be the two lowest, a fresh cut is necessary to decide which of those two deals.

20. Three players cutting cards of equal value cut again ; should the fourth (or remaining) card be the highest, the two lowest of the new cut are partners, the lower of those two the dealer ; should the fourth card be the lowest, the two highest are partners, the original lowest the dealer.

CUTTING OUT

21. At the end of a rubber, should admission be claimed by any one, or by two candidates, he who has, or they who have, played a greater number of consecutive rubbers than the others is, or are, out ; but when all have played the same number, they must cut to decide upon the outgoers ; the highest are out.

Entry and Re-entry

22. A candidate, whether he has played or not, can join a table which is not complete by declaring in at any time prior to any of the players having cut a card, either for the purpose of commencing a fresh rubber or of cutting out.

23. In the formation of fresh tables, those candidates who have neither belonged to nor played at any other table have the prior right of entry; the others decide their right of admission by cutting.

24. Any one quitting a table prior to the conclusion of a rubber, may, with consent of the other three players, appoint a substitute in his absence during that rubber.

25. A player joining one table, whilst belonging to another, loses his right of re-entry into the latter, and takes his chance of cutting in, as if he were a fresh candidate.

26. If any one break up a table, the remaining players have the prior right to him of entry into any other; and should there not be sufficient vacancies at such other table to admit all those candidates, they settle their precedence by cutting.

Shuffling

27. The pack must neither be shuffled below the table nor so that the face of any card be seen.

28. The pack must not be shuffled during the play of the hand.

29. A pack, having been played with, must neither be shuffled by dealing it into packets, nor across the table.

30. Each player has a right to shuffle once only (except as provided by Law 33) prior to a deal, after a false cut, or when a new deal has occurred.

31. The dealer's partner must collect the cards for the ensuing deal, and has the first right to shuffle that pack.

32. Each player, after shuffling, must place the cards, properly collected and face downwards, to the left of the player about to deal.

33. The dealer has always the right to shuffle last; but should a card or cards be seen during

his shuffling, or whilst giving the pack to be cut,
he may be compelled to re-shuffle.

THE DEAL

34. Each player deals in his turn ; the order
of dealing goes to the left.

35. The player on the dealer's right cuts the
pack, and in dividing it, must not leave fewer
than four cards in either packet : if in cutting,
or in replacing one of the two packets on the
other, a card be exposed, or if there be any confusion of the cards, or a doubt as to the exact
place in which the pack was divided, there must
be a fresh cut.

36. When a player, whose duty it is to cut,
has once separated the pack, he cannot alter his
intention ; he can neither re-shuffle nor re-cut
the cards.

37. When the pack is cut, should the dealer
shuffle the cards, the pack must be cut again.

38. The fifty-two cards shall be dealt face
downwards. The deal is not completed until
the last card has been dealt face downwards.
There is no misdeal.

A NEW DEAL

39. There must be a new deal—
   I. If, during a deal, or during the play of a
      hand, the pack be proved to be incor-
      rect or imperfect.
  II. If any card be faced in the pack.
 III. Unless the cards are dealt into four
      packets, one at a time and in regular
      rotation, beginning at the player to the
      dealer's left.
  IV. Should the last card not come in its
      regular order to the dealer.
   V. Should a player have more than thirteen
      cards, and any one or more of the
      others less than thirteen cards.
  VI. Should the dealer deal two cards at once,
      or two cards to the same hand, and
      then deal a third ; but if, prior to
      dealing that card, the dealer can, by
      altering the position of one card only,
      rectify such error, he may do so.
 VII. Should the dealer omit to have the pack
      cut to him, and the adversaries dis-

cover the error prior to the last card being dealt, and before looking at their cards; but not after having done so.

40. If, whilst dealing, a card be exposed by either of the dealer's adversaries, the dealer or his partner may claim a new deal. A card similarly exposed by the dealer or his partner gives the same claim to each adversary. The claim may not be made by a player who has looked at any of his cards. If a new deal does not take place, the exposed card cannot be called.

41. If, in dealing, one of the last cards be exposed, and the dealer completes the deal before there is reasonable time to decide as to a fresh deal, the privilege is not thereby lost.

42. If the dealer, before he has dealt fifty-one cards, look at any card, his adversaries have a right to see it, and may exact a new deal.

43. Should three players have their right number of cards—the fourth have less than thirteen, and not discover such deficiency until he has played any of his cards, the deal stands good; should he have played, he is as answerable for any revoke he may have made as if the missing card, or cards, had been in his hand; he may search the other pack for it, or them.

44. If a pack, during or after a rubber, be proved incorrect or imperfect, such proof does not alter any past score, game, or rubber; that hand in which the imperfection was detected is null and void; the dealer deals again.

45. Any one dealing out of turn, or with the adversary's cards, may be stopped before the last card is dealt, otherwise the deal stands good, and the game must proceed as if no mistake had been made.

46. A player can neither shuffle, cut, nor deal for his partner without the permission of his opponents.

DECLARING TRUMPS

47. The dealer, having examined his hand, has the option of declaring what suit shall be trumps, or whether the hand shall be played without trumps. If he exercise that option, he shall do so by naming the suit, or by saying "No trumps."

48. If the dealer does not wish to exercise his option, he may pass it to his partner by saying, "I leave it to you, Partner," and his partner must thereupon make the necessary declaration, in the manner provided in the preceding law.

49. If the dealer's partner make the trump declaration without receiving permission from the dealer, the eldest hand may demand:

I. That the declaration so made shall stand.

II. That there shall be a new deal.

But if any declaration as to doubling or not doubling shall have been made, or if a new deal is not claimed, the declaration wrongly made shall stand. The eldest hand is the player on the left of the dealer.

50. If the dealer's partner pass the declaration to the dealer, the eldest hand may demand:

I. That there shall be a new deal.

II. That the dealer's partner shall himself make the declaration.

51. If either of the dealer's adversaries make the declaration, the dealer may, after looking at his hand, either claim a fresh deal or proceed as if no such declaration had been made.

52. A declaration once made cannot be altered, save as provided above.

DOUBLING AND RE-DOUBLING

53. The effect of doubling and re-doubling, and so on, is that the value of each trick above six is doubled, quadrupled, and so on.

54. After the trump declaration has been made by the dealer or his partner, their adversaries have the right to double. The eldest hand has the first right. If he does not wish to double, he shall say to his partner, "May I lead?" His partner shall answer, "Yes," or "I double."

55. If either of their adversaries elect to double, the dealer and his partner have the right to re-double. The player who has declared the trump shall have the first right. He may say, "I re-double" or "Satisfied." Should he say the latter, his partner may re-double.

56. If the dealer or his partner elect to re-double, their adversaries shall have the right to again double. The original doubler has the first right.

57. If the right-hand adversary of the dealer

double before his partner has asked " May I lead ? " the declarer of the trump shall have the right to say whether or not the double shall stand. If he decide that the double shall stand, the process of re-doubling may continue as described in Laws 55, 56, 58.

58. The process of re-doubling may be continued until the limit of 100 points is reached—the first right to continue the re-doubling on behalf of a partnership belonging to that player who has last re-doubled. Should he, however, express himself satisfied, the right to continue the re-doubling passes to his partner. Should any player re-double out of turn, the adversary who last doubled shall decide whether or not such double shall stand. If it is decided that the re-double shall stand, the process of re-doubling may continue as described in this and foregoing laws (55 and 56). If any double or re-double out of turn be not accepted there shall be no further doubling in that hand. Any consultation between partners as to doubling or re-doubling will entitle the maker of the trump or the eldest hand, without consultation, to a new deal.

59. If the eldest hand lead before the doubling be completed, his partner may re-double only with the consent of the adversary who last doubled ; but such lead shall not affect the right of either adversary to double.

60. When the question, " May I lead ? " has been answered in the affirmative, or when the player who has the last right to continue the doubling expresses himself satisfied, the play shall begin.

61. A declaration once made cannot be altered.

DUMMY

62. As soon as a card is led, whether in or out of turn, the dealer's partner shall place his cards face upwards on the table, and the duty of playing the cards from that hand, which is called Dummy, and of claiming and enforcing any penalties arising during the hand, shall devolve upon the dealer, unassisted by his partner.

63. After exposing Dummy, the dealer's partner has no part whatever in the game, ex-

cept that he has the right to ask the dealer if he has none of the suit in which he may have renounced. If he call attention to any other incident in the play of the hand, in respect of which any penalty might be exacted, the fact that he has done so shall deprive the dealer of the right of exacting such penalty against his adversaries.

64. If the dealer's partner, by touching a card, or otherwise, suggest the play of a card from Dummy, either of the adversaries may, but without consulting with his partner, call upon the dealer to play or not to play the card suggested.

65. When the dealer draws a card, either from his own hand or from Dummy, such card is not considered as played until actually quitted.

66. A card once played, or named by the dealer as to be played from his own hand or from Dummy, cannot be taken back, except to save a revoke.

67. The dealer's partner may not look over his adversaries' hands, nor leave his seat for the purpose of watching his partner's play.

68. Dummy is not liable to any penalty for a revoke, as his adversaries see his cards. Should he revoke, and the error not be discovered until the trick is turned and quitted, the trick stands good.

69. Dummy being blind and deaf, his partner is not liable to any penalty for an error whence he can gain no advantage. Thus, he may expose some, or all of his cards, without incurring any penalty.

EXPOSED CARDS

70. If after the deal has been completed, and before the trump declaration has been made, either the dealer or his partner expose a card from his hand, the eldest hand may claim a new deal.

71. If after the deal has been completed, and before a card is led, any player shall expose a card, his partner shall forfeit any right to double or re-double which he would otherwise have been entitled to exercise; and in the case of a card being so exposed by the leader's partner, the dealer may, instead of calling the card, require the leader not to lead the suit of the exposed card.

Cards Liable to be Called

72. All cards exposed by the dealer's adversaries are liable to be called, and must be left face upwards on the table ; but a card is not an exposed card when dropped on the floor, or elsewhere below the table.

73. The following are exposed cards :
 I. Two or more cards played at once.
 II. Any card dropped with its face upwards, or in any way exposed on or above the table, even though snatched up so quickly that no one can name it.

74. If either of the dealer's adversaries play to an imperfect trick the best card on the table, or lead one which is a winning card as against the dealer and his partner, and then lead again, without waiting for his partner to play, or play several such winning cards, one after the other, without waiting for his partner to play, the latter may be called on to win, if he can, the first or any other of those tricks, and the other cards thus improperly played are exposed cards.

75. Should the dealer indicate that all or any of the remaining tricks are his, he may be required to place his cards face upwards on the table ; but they are not liable to be called.

76. If either of the dealer's adversaries throws his cards on the table face upwards, such cards are exposed, and liable to be called by the dealer.

77. If all the players throw their cards on the table face upwards, the hands are abandoned, and the score must be left as claimed and admitted. The hands may be examined for the purpose of establishing a revoke, but for no other purpose.

78. A card detached from the rest of the hand of either of the dealer's adversaries, so as to be named, is liable to be called ; but should the dealer name a wrong card, he is liable to have a suit called when first he or his partner have the lead.

79. If a player, who has rendered himself liable to have the highest or lowest of a suit called, or to win or not to win a trick, fail to play as desired, though able to do so, or if when called on to lead one suit, lead another, having in his

hand one or more cards of that suit demanded, he incurs the penalty of a revoke.

80. If either of the dealer's adversaries lead out of turn, the dealer may call a suit from him or his partner when it is next the turn of either of them to lead, or may call the card erroneously led.

81. If the dealer lead out of turn, either from his own hand or from Dummy, he incurs no penalty; but he may not rectify the error after the second hand has played.

82. If any player lead out of turn, and the other three have followed him, the trick is complete, and the error cannot be rectified; but if only the second, or the second and third, have played to the false lead, their cards, on discovery of the mistake, are taken back; and there is no penalty against any one, excepting the original offender, and then only when he is one of the dealer's adversaries.

83. In no case can a player be compelled to play a card which would oblige him to revoke.

84. The call of a card may be repeated until such card has been played.

85. If a player called on to lead a suit have none of it, the penalty is paid.

CARDS PLAYED IN ERROR, OR NOT PLAYED TO A TRICK

86. Should the third hand not have played, and the fourth play before his partner, the latter (not being Dummy or his partner) may be called on to win, or not to win, the trick.

87. If any one (not being Dummy) omit playing to a former trick, and such error be not discovered until he has played to the next, the adversaries may claim a new deal; should they decide that the deal stand good, or should Dummy have omitted to play to a former trick, and such error be not discovered till he shall have played to the next, the surplus card at the end of the hand is considered to have been played to the imperfect trick, but does not constitute a revoke therein.

88. If any one play two cards to the same trick, or mix a card with a trick to which it does not properly belong, and the mistake be not discovered until the hand is played out, he (not

being Dummy) is answerable for all consequent revokes he may have made. If, during the play of the hand, the error be detected, the tricks may be counted face downwards, in order to ascertain whether there be among them a card too many : should this be the case they may be searched, and the card restored ; the player (not being Dummy) is, however, liable for all revokes which he may have meanwhile made.

THE REVOKE

89. Is when a player (other than Dummy), holding one or more cards of the suit led, plays a card of a different suit.

90. The penalty for a revoke—

  I. Is at the option of the adversaries, who, at the end of the hand, may, after consultation, either take three tricks from the revoking player and add them to their own—or deduct the value of three tricks from his existing score—or add the value of three tricks to their own score ;

 II. Can be claimed for as many revokes as occur during the hand ;

III. Is applicable only to the score of the game in which it occurs ;

IV. Cannot be divided—*i.e.* a player cannot add the value of one or two tricks to his own score and deduct the value of one or two from the revoking player.

 V. In whatever way the penalty may be enforced, under no circumstances can the side revoking score Game, Grand Slam, or Little Slam, that hand. Whatever their previous score may be, the side revoking cannot attain a higher score towards the game than twenty-eight.

91. A revoke is established, if the trick in which it occur be turned and quitted—*i.e.* the hand removed from that trick after it has been turned face downwards on the table—or if either the revoking player or his partner, whether in his right turn or otherwise, lead or play to the following trick.

92. A player may ask his partner whether he has not a card of the suit which he has re-

nounced ; should the question be asked before the trick is turned and quitted, subsequent turning and quitting does not establish the revoke, and the error may be corrected, unless the question be answered in the negative, or unless the revoking player or his partner have led or played to the following trick.

93. At the end of the hand, the claimants of a revoke may search all the tricks.

94. If a player discover his mistake in time to save a revoke, any player or players who have played after him may withdraw their cards and substitute others, and their cards withdrawn are not liable to be called. If the player in fault be one of the dealer's adversaries, the dealer may call the card thus played in error, or may require him to play his highest or lowest card to that trick in which he has renounced.

95. If the player in fault be the dealer, the eldest hand may require him to play the highest or lowest card of the suit in which he has renounced, provided both of the dealer's adversaries have played to the current trick ; but this penalty cannot be exacted from the dealer when he is fourth in hand, nor can it be enforced at all from Dummy.

96. If a revoke be claimed, and the accused player or his partner mix the cards before they have been sufficiently examined by the adversaries, the revoke is established. The mixing of the cards only renders the proof of a revoke difficult, but does not prevent the claim, and possible establishment, of the penalty.

97. A revoke cannot be claimed after the cards have been cut for the following deal.

98. If a revoke occur, be claimed and proved, bets on the odd trick, or on amount of score, must be decided by the actual state of the score after the penalty is paid.

99. Should the players on both sides subject themselves to the penalty of one or more revokes, neither can win the game by that hand ; each is punished at the discretion of his adversary.

CALLING FOR NEW CARDS

100. Any player (on paying for them) before, but not after, the pack is cut for the deal, may call for fresh cards. He must call for two new packs, of which the dealer takes his choice.